THIRD EDITION

WALK HUMBLY WITH YOUR GOD

PUTTING GOD'S PURPOSES FIRST IN YOUR LIFE

EDWARD D. ANDREWS

WALK HUMBLY WITH YOUR GOD

Putting God's Purpose First in Your Life

Third Edition

Edward D. Andrews

Christian Publishing House
Cambridge, Ohio

Copyright © 2020 Edward D. Andrews

All rights reserved. Except for brief quotations in articles, other publications, book reviews, and blogs, no part of this book may be reproduced in any manner without prior written permission from the publishers. For information, write, support@christianpublishers.org

WALK HUMBLY WITH YOUR GOD: Putting God's Purpose First in Your Life by Edward D. Andrews

ISBN-13: **978-1-949586-69-5**

ISBN-10: **1-949586-69-3**

Table of Contents

- Book Description 8
- Preface 10
- Introduction 12
- **CHAPTER 1 Walking with God in the Beginning** 14
  - Deepening Our Knowledge 14
  - Our Decision and Dedication to Serve God 16
- **CHAPTER 2 Cause Me to Walk in Your Truth and Teach Me** 20
  - Guided Paths: Learning and Living God's Truth 20
  - Divine Direction: The Pursuit of Spiritual Enlightenment 22
- **CHAPTER 3 Faithfully Walking in the Truth** 25
  - Steadfast Journeys: Upholding Integrity in Faith 25
  - Living Authenticity: The Daily Walk of Truth 27
- **CHAPTER 4 Walk Humbly with Your God** 30
  - The Modesty of Faith: Embracing Humility with the Divine. 30
  - Simplicity in Steps: The Essence of Humble Walking 32
- **CHAPTER 5 Can We Truly Walk with God?** 36
  - The Possibility of Divine Communion: Myth or Reality? 36
  - Within Reach: The Attainable Walk with the Almighty 39
- **CHAPTER 6 Will You Choose to Walk with God?** 43
  - At the Crossroads of Will: Choosing the Path of Faith 43
  - Decision's Journey: The Choice to Walk with the Creator 46
- **CHAPTER 7 Walk with God Even in Times of Difficulty** 50
  - Through Valleys and Shadows: Perseverance in Faith 50
  - Resilient Steps: The Walk of Faith Amidst Life's Storms 53
- **CHAPTER 8 Carry on in Your Walking with God** 57

Enduring the Marathon: Longevity in Your Spiritual Walk ... 57

Unwavering Progress: Continuing Your Path with God 60

CHAPTER 9 Continuously Walking in the Truth............63

Without Cease: The Constant Walk in God's Reality............. 63

Perpetual Motion: Advancing in Truth Every Day................. 66

CHAPTER 10 Examine Yourselves to See Whether You Are in the Faith..69

Self-Reflection: Testing the Authenticity of Faith.................... 69

Faith Under Scrutiny: The Examination of Belief 72

CHAPTER 11 Walking with God in Spite of Doubt 76

Understanding Uncertainty: The Role of Doubt in Faith........ 76

Shadows of Questioning: Defining and Dealing with Doubt 79

CHAPTER 12 Do Not Give Up in Your Walk with God! ..83

The Resolve to Continue: Overcoming Spiritual Fatigue 83

Persevere in Prayer: The Tenacity of Faith 86

CHAPTER 13 Those Who Lack Faith Cannot Walk with God 89

The Necessity of Belief: Foundations for the Journey............. 89

Faithless Wanderings: The Implications of Doubt................... 92

CHAPTER 14 Let Us Never Shrink Back from Our Walk with God 96

Fortified Steps: Standing Firm in Your Spiritual Journey........ 96

Unretractable Faith: The Commitment to Forward Motion .. 99

CHAPTER 15 Christian Way of Life 103

The Path Lived: The Everyday of Christian Living................ 103

Beyond Sundays: Integrating Faith into the Fabric of Life .. 106

CHAPTER 16 Walk in Wisdom Toward Outsiders......... 110

Navigating Relationships: Wisdom in Witness 110

Bridges, Not Barriers: Engaging Others with Grace and Insight 113

CHAPTER 17 'Paying Close Attention as to How We Walk 117

Mindful Steps: The Intentionality of Spiritual Conduct 117

Eyes Wide Open: The Conscious Choice to Walk Uprightly 120

CHAPTER 18 Walk by the Spirit 124

Spirit-Led Steps: Aligning with the Divine Presence 124

Invisible Guidance: The Daily Influence of the Spirit on Our Walk 127

Bibliography 131

Edward D. Andrews

Book Description

In "Walk Humbly with Your God: Putting God's Purpose First in Your Life," readers are invited on a transformative journey to deepen their relationship with God and align their lives with His divine purpose. Through a compelling blend of biblical insight, practical wisdom, and heartfelt conviction, this book serves as a guide to anyone yearning to walk more closely with God.

The chapters unfold a path of spiritual discovery, starting from the roots of our relationship with the Divine in "Walking with God in the Beginning" and moving through the many aspects of a life lived in faith. The book offers a profound look into what it means to truly walk in God's truth, teaching readers to embrace a life guided by divine principles and to maintain integrity in their faith even in the face of adversity.

This profound work delves into the essence of humility in "Walk Humbly with Your God," encouraging readers to cast aside pride and embrace a simpler, more modest approach to their spiritual journey. It grapples with the realities of doubt and difficulty in chapters like "Walking with God in Spite of Doubt" and "Do Not Give Up in Your Walk with God!", providing encouragement and strategies to persevere.

"Walk Humbly with Your God" does not shy away from challenging readers to examine their faith deeply, as seen in chapters like "Examine Yourselves to See Whether You Are in the Faith." It also highlights the importance of wisdom and discernment in dealing with others in "Walk in Wisdom Toward Outsiders," promoting a Christian way of life that extends beyond the walls of the church and into every interaction.

Perhaps most crucially, the book culminates in the profound reflection on the role of the Holy Spirit in our daily walk with God. "Walk by the Spirit" and "Invisible Guidance: The Daily Influence of the Spirit on Our Walk" offer an in-depth understanding of how to live a life that is not only informed by Scripture but also led by the Spirit's gentle guidance.

Each chapter serves as a milestone in the believer's spiritual expedition, from choosing to walk with God, to continuously moving forward in faith, to never shrinking back. "Walk Humbly with Your God" is more than a book; it's a lifelong companion for anyone who seeks to live a life that is pleasing to God, filled with the joy of His presence and the peace of His guidance.

Join the multitude of believers who have found in these pages a roadmap to a richer, more fulfilling relationship with God. Whether at the dawn of your spiritual journey or well along the path, this book is an invaluable resource for anyone seeking to put God's purpose first in their life.

Preface

In the quiet moments of reflection, a question often whispers in the hearts of believers: How does one truly walk with God in the modern world? The answers are as timeless as Scripture and as pertinent as the morning news. "Walk Humbly with Your God: Putting God's Purpose First in Your Life" is not merely a response to this whisper; it is a clarion call to those who seek to live out their faith with authenticity and resolve.

This book has been birthed from a profound and enduring contemplation of the Scriptures, coupled with an unwavering commitment to the unadulterated truths within the Holy Writ. It is an endeavor to knit together the wisdom of ancient biblical texts with the complex threads of contemporary life.

In the chapters that follow, we embark on a journey—an exploration that travels the breadth of human experience, from the peaks of spiritual enlightenment to the valleys of trial and doubt. It is a pilgrimage that invites the reader to stride alongside biblical figures and modern-day believers alike, learning from their walks with God.

The instruction herein does not offer easy steps or shallow promises. Instead, it provides a deep and abiding consideration of what it means to live a life fully surrendered to God, a life that prioritizes His purpose above all else. The chapters are crafted to challenge, inspire, and equip readers to discern the presence of God in every step, to recognize His guidance, and to respond with obedient and humble hearts.

As we consider what it means to walk by the Spirit, we understand that such a walk is not driven by transient feelings or mystical experiences. Rather, it is marked by a conscious, daily decision to align our will with God's revealed Word, acknowledging that while the Holy Spirit does not indwell believers, His influence is powerfully felt through the truths of Scripture that mold and shape our lives.

"Walk Humbly with Your God" is an invitation to journey through life with eyes fixed on the eternal, guided by the ancient texts that speak into our present and illuminate our path. May the pages that follow serve as a trusted guide, offering light on the pathway for all who seek to live a life that is pleasing and acceptable to our Creator.

As the author, I am keenly aware of the responsibility that accompanies the penning of such a book. The content herein is the product of earnest study, fervent prayer, and a heartfelt desire to serve those who seek a closer, more genuine relationship with God. I invite you, dear reader, to turn these pages with anticipation, allowing the Spirit of God, through His Scriptures, to lead you into a deeper understanding and a more faithful walk with our God.

Edward D. Andrews

Author of 220+ books

Introduction

To walk with God: the concept is as ancient as the garden of Eden and as current as today's quest for meaning in a tumultuous world. The idea evokes a companionship with the Divine that is both intimate and reverent, a relationship that many earnestly long to comprehend and experience. Yet, it remains elusive to many, shrouded in misconceptions and sometimes obscured by the clamor of conflicting voices.

"Walk Humbly with Your God: Putting God's Purpose First in Your Life" is more than a textual endeavor; it is a spiritual expedition designed to navigate the intricate interplay between divine precepts and human existence. The aim of this introduction is to set the stage for a transformative engagement with God's Word, providing a roadmap for the enriching journey that lies within these pages.

As you turn these pages, you will not find a passive reading experience, but rather an active engagement with the living Scriptures. Each chapter serves as a stepping stone toward a fuller, richer understanding of what it means to live according to the will and wisdom of God. We will venture through the gardens of biblical teaching, pause at the wellsprings of divine wisdom, and ascend the high places of spiritual commitment.

This introduction, then, is an invitation to enter the journey with an open heart and a willing spirit, ready to explore the depths of your relationship with God. Whether you are taking the first steps toward faith or have been walking the path of belief for decades, there is a place for you in these pages.

The journey of walking with God is marked not by a pursuit of fleeting emotional experiences but by a steadfast commitment to grow in understanding and obedience to God's Word. It is a walk characterized by humility, where the grandeur of God's purposes eclipses our own, and where our daily choices reflect the value we place on spiritual truths over temporal distractions.

The chapters ahead do not promise a life free from challenge or doubt; rather, they acknowledge the reality of these experiences as part of the fabric of faith. Herein, we will discover how to walk with God even when the path is obscured by the shadows of difficulty, and how to maintain our course when the way seems arduous.

"Walk Humbly with Your God" invites you to step into a journey that is both personal and communal, an exploration of faith that honors the past, engages the present, and anticipates the future. As your guide, I am committed to presenting you with a clear, faithful, and robust exposition of the Scriptures, fostering a walk with God that is deeply rooted in biblical truth and lived out with conviction and purpose.

Welcome to the journey. May it lead you to walk humbly with your God, finding His purpose for your life as you do so.

Edward D. Andrews

CHAPTER 1 Walking with God in the Beginning

Deepening Our Knowledge

In the transformative journey of walking with God, the initial steps a new Christian takes are crucial. It is here, in these first moments of newfound faith, where the foundation is laid for a lifetime of walking humbly with our Creator. For those who have recently come to accept Christ, it is imperative to begin with a clear understanding of what it means to walk with God and how to deepen that relationship progressively.

Walking with God is a rich phrase that calls to mind the patriarch Enoch, who "walked with God; and he was not, for God took him" (Genesis 5:24 UASV). This early example sets a precedent for what it means to walk with God: living in a way that is pleasing to Him, leading to an intimate and sustained communion with God. For a new believer, this walk begins with the crucial step of *acknowledgment*. Acknowledging that Jesus Christ is Lord and believing that God raised Him from the dead is the key that unlocks the door to a righteous path (Romans 10:9).

Once this door is opened, deepening one's knowledge is not merely about accumulating information but about transformation. This transformation is facilitated by a consistent, humble submission to God's Word and an earnest desire to apply it personally. To understand the Bible, one must approach it with the historical-grammatical method of interpretation, which seeks to discover the text's original meaning in its original context. By doing so, the new believer anchors their understanding in the objective truth of Scripture.

As a new Christian grows in faith, they begin to see the Scriptures not as a collection of distant stories, but as God's living and active word (Hebrews 4:12). This word is not merely for knowledge's sake, but for guiding one's thoughts, actions, and decisions daily. The Bible becomes a mirror reflecting the areas in one's life that require change and is also the map that guides that change.

For example, consider the new Christian grappling with pride. James 4:6 reminds us that "God opposes the proud but gives grace to the humble." In this, the new believer learns that to walk with God, one must practice humility—a quality not naturally ingrained in the human disposition. By meditating on this scripture, recognizing personal prideful tendencies, and actively seeking to emulate the humility of Christ, the individual aligns more closely with God's will.

Engagement with Scripture naturally leads to prayer. Prayer is the vital communication with God that enables the believer to express their deepest concerns, confess their sins, and seek guidance. It is also the means by which they offer thanks and praise to God for His goodness and mercy. As the Psalmist wrote, "The sacrifice acceptable to God is a broken spirit; a broken and contrite heart, O God, you will not despise" (Psalm 51:17). In prayer, the believer approaches God with a heart willing to be molded, and it is here where intimate knowledge of God's character and will is deepened.

Another concrete step in deepening one's walk with God is through *fellowship with other believers*. The early Christian community, as seen in the book of Acts, thrived on mutual support, teaching, and worship. This communal aspect of the faith is not incidental; it is essential. The new believer is encouraged to become part of a community of faith that prioritizes the accurate teaching of God's Word, allowing them to grow under the mentorship of mature Christians.

Engaging in *service* is another avenue through which a new Christian can deepen their knowledge of God. Service is an expression of love for God and for one's neighbor. It is a practical outworking of faith. In serving others, the new believer imitates Christ, who "came not to be served but to serve" (Matthew 20:28). Whether it is helping at a local shelter, participating in a church clean-up, or simply offering a listening ear to a friend in need, service is a tangible expression of God's love through the believer.

It is equally important for the new Christian to learn the value of *obedience*. This is not the pursuit of perfection but a genuine effort to live according to God's commandments. As they learn God's statutes, new believers will inevitably stumble, but 1 John 1:9 provides assurance that "If we confess our sins, he is faithful and just to forgive us our sins and to cleanse us from all unrighteousness." The practice of repentance and the experience of God's forgiveness deepen the believer's understanding of God's grace and mercy.

Lastly, the new Christian must embrace a *Biblically-informed worldview*. This means interpreting life's experiences, challenges, and cultural trends through the lens of Scripture. It is about forming attitudes and opinions that are grounded in biblical truth rather than personal or societal norms. For instance, when faced with contemporary moral dilemmas, the believer returns to the Bible to understand what is good and acceptable and perfect in God's eyes (Romans 12:2).

In conclusion, to walk with God is to embark on a path of ever-increasing intimacy with God, grounded in the truth of His Word. For the new believer, this path involves a transformation of the heart and mind, led by the Holy Spirit through Scripture. It is a path marked by prayer, fellowship, service, obedience, and a worldview that honors God above all. This journey is not one of isolation but is to be traveled within the community of faith, with eyes fixed on Jesus, the "author and perfecter of our faith" (Hebrews 12:2). As the new Christian grows in their understanding of who God is and what He desires, they will indeed be walking humbly with their God.

Our Decision and Dedication to Serve God

The journey of walking with God is one that demands a conscious decision and an unwavering dedication to serve Him. This choice is the bedrock upon which a believer's faith is built and continually grows. To serve God is not merely a verbal assertion but a life-altering commitment that encompasses every aspect of one's being.

Making the decision to serve God is rooted in the understanding of what God has done through Jesus Christ. It is acknowledging that while "the wages of sin is death," the free gift of God is "eternal life in Christ Jesus our Lord" (Romans 6:23). This realization propels the believer to respond in service, moved by gratitude and love. However, this service is not to be seen as a means to earn favor but as a fruit of one's salvation.

Dedication to serve God means putting God first, before personal desires and ambitions. It is exemplified in the life of Jesus, who said, "not as I will, but as you will" (Matthew 26:39). The decision to serve God, therefore, involves a deliberate orientation of one's life towards God's will and purposes. It is choosing to value what God values, to prioritize what He prioritizes, and to find one's deepest joy and satisfaction in His pleasure.

This dedication is also about constancy. In a world where loyalties shift quickly and commitments are often fleeting, serving God requires steadfastness. The Book of Daniel narrates the story of Shadrach, Meshach, and Abednego, whose dedication to God was tested in the fire—literally. Their unwavering commitment to not serve other gods is a vivid depiction of what dedication in the face of trial looks like.

The Psalms frequently echo the sentiment of dedication to serve God. "I will praise you, O Lord my God, with all my heart, and I will glorify your name forevermore" (Psalm 86:12). Such a pledge is comprehensive; it involves the intellect, emotions, and will. Serving God with all one's heart means that one's intellectual pursuits, emotional energy, and decisions are aligned with the desire to honor God.

Discipleship is a key aspect of this dedication. It involves learning from and following Jesus as Master and Teacher. It is not a passive relationship; it is active and dynamic. As a disciple, the believer adopts a lifestyle that mirrors that of Christ, embracing His teachings and applying them in daily life. When Peter and Andrew were called, they left their nets immediately to follow Jesus (Matthew 4:19-20). Their decision was instant, but their dedication was proved over a lifetime of service.

Furthermore, dedication to God involves a commitment to personal *holiness*. Holiness is often misunderstood as a state of moral superiority, but in its biblical sense, it simply means being set apart for God's use. It is a daily pursuit that affects how one speaks, acts, and thinks. Paul's exhortation to the Romans to present their bodies "as a living sacrifice, holy and pleasing to God" (Romans 12:1) encapsulates this idea. It is an ongoing process, where the believer, empowered by the Holy Spirit, continually turns away from sin and towards God.

The decision to serve God also leads to the believer's active involvement in *witnessing*. This is not just the work of evangelists but the calling of every Christian. The new believer learns to articulate their faith, sharing the reason for their hope with gentleness and respect (1 Peter 3:15). This is not about conversion rates but about faithful representation of Christ's love and truth to others. Witnessing may take many forms; it could be through words, acts of kindness, or simply living a life that raises questions about the hope that the believer possesses.

Sacrifice is an inherent part of this dedication. There are countless biblical examples of sacrifice, from Abraham's willingness to offer Isaac, illustrating ultimate faith and obedience, to the Macedonian churches giving generously out of their poverty (2 Corinthians 8:1-5). The believer learns that serving God often means giving up personal comfort, resources, and even one's plans for the sake of God's purposes.

In the midst of dedication, it is vital to recognize the role of *Scripture* in guiding and nurturing the believer's commitment. Through regular study and meditation on the Word, the believer equips themselves to serve God effectively. Psalm 119:105 affirms, "Your word is a lamp to my feet and a light to my path." The Scriptures provide the wisdom and insight necessary for navigating life's complexities while remaining faithful to God.

Service to God is not without its challenges. There will be moments of doubt, weariness, and even failure. However, dedication is not proven in perfection but in persistence. When the prophet Elijah felt overwhelmed and fled to Horeb, Jehovah met him there, not in the wind, earthquake, or fire, but in a low whisper (1 Kings 19:11-13).

It was a gentle reminder that God does not abandon His servants in their moments of weakness.

Prayer is the lifeline of dedication. It is through prayer that the believer maintains their connection with God, seeking His strength, wisdom, and guidance. The Apostle Paul encourages believers to "pray without ceasing" (1 Thessalonians 5:17), indicating that prayer is to be a constant, not sporadic, part of the Christian life.

In essence, the decision and dedication to serve God are not a one-time act but a lifelong pursuit. It is a journey marked by learning, growth, sacrifice, and above all, love for God. As the believer dedicates their life to serving God, they can truly walk humbly with Him, fulfilling the purpose for which they were created.

CHAPTER 2 Cause Me to Walk in Your Truth and Teach Me

Guided Paths: Learning and Living God's Truth

Embarking on a spiritual journey requires more than just a yearning to walk with God; it necessitates a commitment to learning and living His truth. The quest for understanding God's Word is not a passive reception of information but an active, intentional pursuit that shapes one's entire life.

The psalmist's plea, "Teach me your way, O Jehovah; I will walk in your truth; unite my heart to fear your name" (Psalm 86:11), captures the essence of this pursuit. It is a request for guidance and an acknowledgment of the need for God's truth to permeate the heart, leading to a unified and devoted life of reverence toward Jehovah.

Learning God's truth begins with a recognition of the nature of Scripture itself. The Bible is not a mere collection of ancient texts, but the living Word of God, "sharper than any two-edged sword" (Hebrews 4:12). It is through this Word that God reveals His character, His will, and His plan for humanity. When one approaches the Bible, it is not as a passive reader, but as a student sitting at the feet of the Divine Teacher.

Living God's truth, on the other hand, is the practical application of what one learns. It is James who reminds us to be "doers of the word, and not hearers only" (James 1:22). Knowledge of God's Word that does not transform one's life is like a mirror that reflects an image momentarily before being forgotten. To live out God's truth is to allow it to shape one's decisions, actions, and entire way of being.

The path of learning begins with regular, diligent study. Just as the Bereans examined the Scriptures daily to see if what Paul said was true (Acts 17:11), so should the believer approach the Word with eagerness and scrutiny. This study is not merely academic; it is devotional and personal. It involves asking Jehovah to open one's eyes "that [one] may behold wondrous things out of your law" (Psalm 119:18).

Understanding God's truth requires more than surface reading; it calls for meditation and reflection. The process is similar to that of a tree planted by streams of water, which yields its fruit in season and whose leaf does not wither (Psalm 1:2-3). The tree absorbs the nutrients and water, allowing them to flow into every branch and leaf. Similarly, the believer must absorb the truth of God's Word, allowing it to flow into every aspect of life.

As one grows in understanding, the heart and mind begin to align with God's ways. The prophet Isaiah declares, "For my thoughts are not your thoughts, neither are your ways my ways, declares Jehovah" (Isaiah 55:8). To walk in God's truth is to adopt His thoughts and ways as one's own, a process that requires humility and willingness to change.

Living God's truth also means embodying the principles of Scripture in one's relationships. Paul's letter to the Ephesians outlines how believers are to interact with one another, with instructions rooted in love, truth, and mutual edification (Ephesians 4:25-32). In practice, this looks like a community of believers who speak the truth in love, forgive as they have been forgiven, and build each other up according to their needs.

God's truth is not static; it is transformative. When the Word of God dwells in a person richly, it leads to a life of worship and gratitude (Colossians 3:16). Worship, in this context, is not confined to songs and prayers but is a life lived in obedience and service to God. Gratitude becomes the posture of the heart, recognizing that every good and perfect gift is from above (James 1:17).

The process of learning and living God's truth is also marked by *prayer*. The believer engages in continual dialogue with God, seeking wisdom (James 1:5), asking for understanding, and requesting the strength to apply God's truth in daily living. It is through prayer that the believer maintains an intimate relationship with God, ensuring that the journey of learning and living His truth is not walked alone.

Furthermore, living out God's truth necessitates a commitment to *moral integrity*. Integrity is the consistency between what one believes and how one behaves. Proverbs 10:9 states, "Whoever walks in integrity walks securely, but he who makes his ways crooked will be found out." The believer is called to walk blamelessly and do what is right, as David commits in Psalm 15.

The community of faith plays a significant role in this journey as well. Believers are encouraged to stimulate one another to love and good deeds, not neglecting to meet together, as is the habit of some (Hebrews 10:24-25). The church is not just a support system; it is a living organism, where each member contributes to the growth of the whole in love (Ephesians 4:16).

In summary, guided paths of learning and living God's truth are not for the faint-hearted. They require a steadfast spirit, a diligent mind, and a compassionate heart. As one delves into the depths of God's Word and allows it to shape one's life, one finds that walking in truth is not a burdensome task but the pathway to true freedom (John 8:32). This transformative process brings the believer into closer communion with God and empowers them to walk humbly with their God, reflecting His light and truth in a world that desperately needs it.

Divine Direction: The Pursuit of Spiritual Enlightenment

The pursuit of spiritual enlightenment within the Christian context is a journey that is as personal as it is profound. This pursuit is anchored in the belief that God, through His Word and Spirit, provides the guidance necessary for one to understand and live out His divine purpose. Enlightenment in this vein is not an esoteric or mystical experience but the illumination of the mind and heart by the truths of Scripture, leading to a transformation of life that reflects the character and will of God.

This pursuit begins with the recognition of Scripture as the primary means by which Jehovah communicates His will to humanity.

The psalmist declares, "Your word is a lamp to my feet and a light to my path" (Psalm 119:105). The metaphor of light here is significant; it implies clarity, direction, and the dispelling of darkness. As one delves into the Scriptures, the Holy Spirit works to enlighten the mind, enabling the believer to understand and apply God's truths to their life.

Personal devotion and *study of the Scriptures* are indispensable in this journey. Consider the example of Daniel, who, while in Babylon, set his mind to understand the writings and prophecies concerning his people (Daniel 9:2). His diligent study was accompanied by prayer and fasting, showing a deep longing to grasp the mind of Jehovah regarding the future of Israel. Through this process, God revealed profound truths to Daniel, giving him insight that would comfort and guide many.

The journey of spiritual enlightenment is not a solitary one. The early church exemplified a community that devoted itself to the apostles' teaching and to fellowship (Acts 2:42). This communal aspect of enlightenment suggests that while personal study is vital, the insights gained from collective study and discussion can further illuminate the truths of Scripture.

Prayer is another crucial component of seeking divine direction. It is through prayer that believers communicate with God, express their desires for understanding, and seek the wisdom promised in James 1:5, "If any of you lacks wisdom, let him ask God, who gives generously to all without reproach, and it will be given him." Prayer is not a mere ritual; it is the believer's lifeline to the divine, an act of dependence on God for enlightenment and direction.

Meditation on God's Word goes hand in hand with study and prayer. It involves not only reading the Scriptures but also pondering them, turning them over in one's mind, and asking reflective questions. It is through meditation that the words of Jehovah move from the page into the heart, transforming belief into action. Joshua 1:8 underscores the importance of this practice: "This Book of the Law shall not depart from your mouth, but you shall meditate on it day and night, so that you may be careful to do according to all that is written in it."

The *application of Scriptural principles* in one's daily life is the evidence of true enlightenment. It is not enough to accumulate knowledge; the knowledge must lead to a life that exemplifies the virtues and values of the kingdom of God. The epistles of Paul, especially to the Ephesians and Colossians, are rich with exhortations to live out the new life in Christ, shedding the old self with its practices and putting on the new self, created after the likeness of God in true righteousness and holiness (Ephesians 4:22-24).

Spiritual enlightenment is also accompanied by *fruitfulness*. As one grows in the knowledge and understanding of God's will, their life begins to produce the fruit of the Spirit, which includes love, joy, peace, patience, kindness, goodness, faithfulness, gentleness, and self-control (Galatians 5:22-23). These qualities are not self-generated; they are the result of the Spirit's work in the life of one who is walking in the truth of God's Word.

Furthermore, spiritual enlightenment leads to a *deepened sense of purpose*. As believers come to understand God's overarching narrative of redemption and their part within it, their lives take on a new significance. They recognize that they are not mere spectators in the cosmic drama but active participants in God's redemptive plan. This is reminiscent of Esther, who, understanding the grave situation her people were in, embraced her role, recognizing that she had come to her royal position "for such a time as this" (Esther 4:14).

The pursuit of spiritual enlightenment is also marked by a growing *sensitivity to God's guidance*. This sensitivity is beautifully illustrated in the story of Samuel, who as a boy learned to discern the voice of Jehovah (1 Samuel 3). In like manner, as one's understanding deepens, they become more attuned to the leading of the Spirit, recognizing His prompting, correction, and encouragement in their daily lives.

In conclusion, the divine direction is a process that unfolds progressively as one commits to studying Scripture, engaging in prayer, meditating on God's Word, applying biblical principles, and bearing spiritual fruit. It is a journey that transforms the believer, shaping them into an instrument for God's glory and purposes. As believers walk this path, they experience the fulfillment that comes from living in alignment with the Creator's design, demonstrating that the pursuit of spiritual enlightenment is not only about personal growth but about coming to reflect the very character of God in the world.

CHAPTER 3 Faithfully Walking in the Truth

Steadfast Journeys: Upholding Integrity in Faith

In the Christian walk, integrity is the bedrock upon which a steadfast journey is built. Upholding integrity in faith means consistently aligning one's actions with the truth of Scripture, regardless of the circumstances. This steadfastness is not merely about dogged adherence to a set of rules; it's about cultivating a character that reflects the faithfulness and righteousness of God.

Integrity is a term that, at its core, signifies wholeness and undividedness. To walk with integrity is to be the same person in private as one is in public, the same in adversity as in prosperity. It is a biblical principle that finds its roots in the very nature of Jehovah, who is described as perfect in faithfulness (Deuteronomy 32:4). The psalmist aspired to this divine attribute when he prayed, "Teach me your way, O Jehovah, that I may walk in your truth; unite my heart to fear your name" (Psalm 86:11). The unified heart is a heart of integrity.

Walking in truth necessitates a commitment to *honesty*. Ananias and Sapphira, whose story is told in Acts 5, serve as a sobering example of the consequences of forsaking honesty. Their pretense of generosity, while secretly holding back a portion of their proceeds, was not just a lie to the apostles but to the Holy Spirit. Their lack of integrity in their faith was not only spiritually destructive but physically fatal. Honesty, then, is not simply about avoiding lies but about living a life that is transparent before God and people.

Moral courage is an essential element of integrity. It takes courage to stand for truth when deception is the norm, to hold to moral principles when compromise is convenient, and to confess Christ when silence is safe. The Bible commends the courage of Shadrach,

Meshach, and Abednego, who, faced with the fiery furnace, refused to bow to Nebuchadnezzar's idol (Daniel 3). Their physical deliverance was miraculous, but the true triumph was their unwavering integrity in the face of death.

In the pursuit of integrity, *consistency* in one's faith is key. James speaks of the double-minded man as unstable in all his ways (James 1:8). The double-minded person is one who vacillates between the world's values and God's truth. In contrast, the person of integrity is like a tree planted by streams of water, which yields its fruit in season and whose leaf does not wither (Psalm 1:3). Their consistent faithfulness is evident in every season of life.

Humility also undergirds integrity. It was the tax collector, standing afar off, who would not even lift his eyes to heaven, but beat his breast, saying, 'God, be merciful to me, a sinner!' who was justified rather than the Pharisee who boasted of his religious deeds (Luke 18:13-14). The humility shown here is a recognition of one's need for God's mercy, and it is this posture of heart that maintains the integrity of one's faith.

Endurance in trials is a further reflection of integrity. The apostle Paul speaks of his own hardships as moments when he carried in his body the death of Jesus, so that the life of Jesus may also be manifested in his body (2 Corinthians 4:10). For Paul, these trials did not compromise his integrity but rather confirmed it, demonstrating the power of Christ within him.

Upholding integrity in faith is not just about what one avoids—sin and moral failure—but also about what one embraces. It involves the active pursuit of *good works*. The book of Titus reminds believers to be zealous for good works (Titus 2:14), not to earn salvation, which is a gift of grace, but as a natural outgrowth of a faith that is alive and genuine.

A steadfast journey of faith is a balanced one. It recognizes that *justice, mercy, and faithfulness* are the weightier matters of the law (Matthew 23:23). These are not checkboxes to be marked but qualities to be woven into the fabric of one's daily life.

To uphold integrity in faith is to live a life that is congruent with the gospel. It is to walk in a manner worthy of the calling to which one has been called, with all humility and gentleness, with patience, bearing with one another in love (Ephesians 4:1-2). Such a walk is not about perfection but about authenticity and growth.

In sum, upholding integrity in faith is to commit to a path where one's life—thoughts, words, and actions—is increasingly aligned with the will and Word of God. It is a journey marked by truth, courage, consistency, humility, endurance, good works, justice, mercy, and faithfulness. As one walks this path, the light of one's integrity shines before others, not to glorify oneself, but to glorify God, who calls each believer to this steadfast journey.

Living Authenticity: The Daily Walk of Truth

Living a life of authenticity as a Christian means aligning one's daily walk with the truths of Scripture, cultivating a life that is genuine and free from pretense or hypocrisy. It is in the regular rhythm of daily living that one's true character is formed and demonstrated. The pursuit of an authentic faith is not a once-off endeavor but a continuous process, much like the Israelites gathering manna each morning—daily sustenance from Jehovah (Exodus 16:21).

The fabric of an authentic Christian life is woven with the threads of *daily choices*. These choices may seem mundane, like the decision to speak truthfully in a business deal, or to extend forgiveness to someone who has wronged us. Consider the example of Joseph, who, despite being wrongfully imprisoned, remained faithful to God, refusing to succumb to despair or bitterness (Genesis 39:20-23). His consistent choices in adversity upheld his integrity and bore witness to his authentic faith.

Engaging in *daily Scripture reading* and *prayer* is vital for maintaining authenticity. Just as the Bereans examined the Scriptures daily to see if what Paul said was true (Acts 17:11), believers must also delve into the Bible, allowing God's word to shape their thoughts and actions. Prayer, likewise, is not just a spiritual exercise but a lifeline that connects the believer to the divine, much like the branches that must remain in the vine to bear fruit (John 15:4-5).

The *daily testimony* of a Christian is a powerful instrument of God's truth. Living an authentic life means that one's faith is not hidden but visible through acts of love and good works. It's exemplified in the story of Dorcas, who was known for her good works and acts of charity (Acts 9:36). Her life spoke of her faith in a tangible and impactful way.

Authenticity also involves *daily repentance and self-examination*. King David's plea after his sin with Bathsheba, "Create in me a clean heart, O God, and renew a steadfast spirit within me" (Psalm 51:10), reflects the understanding that walking in truth requires a heart that is continually turned towards God, seeking His renewal.

Authentic relationships within the Christian community are another daily aspect of walking in truth. The New Testament church's sharing and support of one another, as seen in Acts 2:44-47, exemplifies the unity and authenticity expected within the body of Christ. In an authentic community, believers are encouraged to bear one another's burdens (Galatians 6:2), promoting growth and mutual edification.

Daily obedience to God's commands is a clear indicator of living authentically. Jesus said, "If you love me, you will keep my commandments" (John 14:15). Obedience is not about legalism or earning favor but is the natural outflow of love and gratitude towards God. It is the practical application of faith in everyday situations.

Engaging in *daily worship*, whether through song, prayer, service, or simply in the way one conducts their life, is a testament to an authentic relationship with Jehovah. As the psalmist declares, "I will bless Jehovah at all times; his praise shall continually be in my mouth" (Psalm 34:1). Authentic worship transcends a set time and place and becomes a lifestyle.

Confronting *daily challenges and adversities* with faith and trust in God also marks the path of authenticity. The Apostle Paul's hardships, detailed in 2 Corinthians 11:23-29, were met with resilience and trust in God's power. His tribulations did not define his faith but refined it, proving its genuineness.

The *daily labor* in one's vocation is also a testament to an authentic Christian life. The Proverbs 31 woman is praised not just for her fear of Jehovah but for her diligence and industriousness (Proverbs 31:30-31). The manner in which Christians conduct themselves in their work is a reflection of their reverence for God.

In all these aspects, *authenticity* is a daily commitment to being genuine in one's faith, transparent before God and others, and consistent in living out the truths of Scripture. It is not about perfection, but about a sincere effort to walk in the light, as God is in the light, having fellowship with one another, and the blood of Jesus, his Son, cleansing us from all sin (1 John 1:7).

Thus, the daily walk of truth is not characterized by grandiose gestures but by quiet, consistent faithfulness in the face of life's complexities. It is a journey marked by the pursuit of holiness, the exercise of faith, the expression of love, and the demonstration of God's truth in every facet of life. This walk is not without its challenges, but it is sustained by the grace and strength that comes from a deep, personal relationship with God, whose guidance and wisdom are ever-present and whose purposes for our lives are good and perfect (Romans 12:2).

Edward D. Andrews

CHAPTER 4 Walk Humbly with Your God

The Modesty of Faith: Embracing Humility with the Divine

Humility is an often misunderstood and overlooked virtue in the fabric of faith, yet it is central to a genuine relationship with the Divine. It is not about self-deprecation or weakness; rather, it is the modesty of faith—a recognition of our rightful place before Jehovah and an acknowledgment of His greatness and sovereignty.

In the biblical narrative, Moses is described as "very humble, more than any man who was on the face of the earth" (Numbers 12:3). This was not because Moses had a low opinion of himself; he was aware of his capabilities and acted with authority when needed. His humility lay in his relationship with Jehovah, with an unassuming nature that made him teachable and obedient to divine direction. Moses' encounter with Jehovah at the burning bush is an illustrative moment of this humility (Exodus 3). Here, Moses takes off his sandals in recognition of the sanctity of God's presence, a gesture of reverence and submission.

Humility is also about seeing ourselves in the light of Jehovah's holiness and our own sinfulness. Isaiah's vision in Isaiah 6 is a profound example. When Isaiah sees Jehovah, he exclaims, "Woe is me, for I am undone; because I am a man of unclean lips" (Isaiah 6:5). It is a moment of honest self-assessment in the light of God's purity. Similarly, the publican in Jesus' parable who beats his breast and says, "God, be merciful to me a sinner," illustrates the humility that recognizes personal inadequacy and seeks divine mercy (Luke 18:13).

Humility is also reflected in the willingness to serve others, following the example of Christ. Jesus washed the feet of his disciples, a task typically reserved for the lowest servant, as a demonstration of humble service (John 13:1-17). He explains that true greatness in the kingdom of God is not found in lordship and authority but in service and humility.

The virtue of humility is fundamental in prayer and worship. When King Solomon dedicates the temple, he kneels in front of all the assembly of Israel—a display of humility not just before Jehovah but before the people he leads (2 Chronicles 6:13). It is a public act of humbling oneself before God, recognizing His supremacy and the need for His presence among His people.

Humility is necessary for learning and growth in faith. Proverbs 11:2 states, "When pride comes, then comes disgrace, but with the humble is wisdom." A humble person is open to correction and instruction, like Apollos, who "began to speak boldly in the synagogue," but when Priscilla and Aquila heard him, they took him aside and "explained to him the way of God more accurately" (Acts 18:26). Apollos received their counsel and continued his ministry, better equipped to teach the truth.

Furthermore, humility is a safeguard against the deception of pride. The Pharisee who prays thanking God that he is not like other men is contrasted with the tax collector who pleads for mercy. Jesus concludes that it was the latter who went home justified before God (Luke 18:14). It is a reminder that self-righteousness is antithetical to true faith, which is grounded in a humble recognition of one's need for God's grace.

Humility also influences how we approach God's Word. A humble heart does not twist the Scriptures to fit personal desires or preconceived notions but approaches God's Word with a readiness to hear, accept, and apply it as truth. James 1:21 encourages believers to "receive with meekness the implanted word, which is able to save your souls." It is through a posture of humility that the transformative power of God's Word takes full effect in our lives.

In living out our faith, humility impacts our relationships with others. It is not passive; it actively seeks the good of others over personal ambition or vanity. Philippians 2:3-4 instructs believers to "do nothing from selfish ambition or conceit, but in humility count others more significant than yourselves." This echoes the mind of Christ, who, though He was in the form of God, did not count equality with God a thing to be grasped, but emptied Himself, taking the form of a servant (Philippians 2:6-7).

Finally, embracing humility with the Divine shapes our perspective on life and its circumstances. Understanding that "Jehovah is near to the brokenhearted and saves the crushed in spirit" (Psalm 34:18) can bring comfort in trials. It assures that Jehovah does not disregard the humble but provides grace sufficient for their needs (2 Corinthians 12:9). In adversity, a humble trust in Jehovah's sovereignty and goodness sustains the believer, much like Job, who despite his suffering, did not charge God with wrong (Job 1:22).

In summary, the modesty of faith is not in grandiose statements or flamboyant displays of piety. It is in the quiet, daily walk of truth that humbly aligns one's heart with the heart of Jehovah. It is in the understanding that He is the potter and we are the clay, and in His hands, we find our purpose and our peace (Isaiah 64:8). The journey of faith, walked in humility before the Divine, is a journey of profound depth, marked by an enduring trust in the One who calls us to "walk humbly with your God" (Micah 6:8). This walk is neither a sprint nor a solitary endeavor but a steady, lifelong pilgrimage alongside the shepherd of our souls (1 Peter 2:25).

Simplicity in Steps: The Essence of Humble Walking

Walking humbly with God does not necessitate extraordinary feats or profound theological knowledge; it is found in the simplicity of daily living, with each step taken in submission to Jehovah's will. It is a journey marked not by complexity and fanfare, but by the pure, straightforward pursuit of godliness—a simplicity in steps.

This simplicity is rooted in a life uncluttered by the world's distractions, where one's focus is sharply tuned to the divine. It resonates with David's single-hearted request in Psalm 27:4, "One thing have I asked of Jehovah, that will I seek after: that I may dwell in the house of Jehovah all the days of my life, to gaze upon the beauty of Jehovah and to inquire in his temple." David's longing for God's presence above all else underscores the essence of a life uncomplicated by competing loyalties.

The Practice of Presence

The essence of humble walking is the practice of God's presence in the mundane. It is to imitate Jesus, who "increased in wisdom and in stature and in favor with God and man" (Luke 2:52). His life, a tapestry of simple yet profound obedience, was a consistent walk in alignment with His Father's will, from the simplicity of carpentry to the profundity of teaching in the temple. Similarly, believers are called to find holiness in the ordinary, recognizing that every action done in faith is an act of worship.

The Subtlety of Obedience

Obedience in simplicity is often quiet and unassuming. Consider Ruth, who in her loyalty and service to Naomi, reflects a life of simple, humble steps (Ruth 1:16-17). Her subsequent gleaning in the fields, a task both modest and necessary, positions her to receive Boaz's favor, illustrating how Jehovah honors the humble obedience found in everyday faithfulness.

The Uncomplicated Pursuit of Righteousness

The pursuit of righteousness, too, is inherent in humble walking. It is not an esoteric quest, but a practical, daily commitment to upright living. This is reflected in the life of Daniel, who, even in the complex political environment of Babylon, maintained consistent integrity and devotion to Jehovah (Daniel 1:8). His resolve to avoid defilement by the king's food is a telling example of steadfastness in simple matters that honor God.

The Clarity of Decision-Making

Simplicity in steps affords clarity in decision-making. It avoids the paralysis often brought on by over-analysis or the temptation to rely solely on human wisdom. The early church's decision regarding

Gentile believers, found in Acts 15, demonstrates the wisdom that comes from seeking God's will in simplicity. The apostles and elders, with the whole church, looked to the Scriptures and the guiding principles of faith to arrive at their resolution, favoring a burden-free invitation to faith for the Gentiles.

The Peace of a Focused Life

A focused life, undistracted by the complexities of the world, allows for a peace that is not easily disturbed. Philippians 4:11-13 reveals Paul's secret to contentment: living in simplicity regardless of circumstances. His ability to be content in any situation—whether in abundance or need—is a direct result of his simple trust in Christ who strengthens him.

The Simplicity of Worship

Worship in its most profound form is simple; it does not rely on the ostentatious or the elaborate but emerges from a heart aligned with God's heart. The early believers' breaking of bread and prayers, as described in Acts 2:42, show a simplicity in communal worship that is powerful and transformative. Their gathering was not marked by elaborate ritual but by a shared devotion and simplicity of heart.

The Stewardship of Resources

In humble walking, there is also simplicity in the stewardship of resources. The Macedonian believers, though in extreme poverty, gave generously to support their fellow believers, a profound demonstration of grace and willingness (2 Corinthians 8:1-5). Their simple yet sacrificial giving is a model of stewardship that prioritizes God's kingdom and reflects a heart of worship.

The Authenticity of Relationships

Humble walking fosters authenticity in relationships. The straightforward love and correction Paul extends to the Corinthian church is indicative of the unfeigned relationships that should characterize the body of Christ (1 Corinthians 4:14-21). Such transparency and simplicity in relational dealings build up the church in truth and love.

The Discipline of Simplicity

A disciplined approach to simplicity helps in eschewing the superfluous and in cultivating a life of substance and depth. As Jesus taught through parables, using simple stories to convey deep truths, believers too are to distill the essence of godly living into their daily routines, relationships, and decisions.

In conclusion, the essence of humble walking is found in the simplicity of a life focused on God, practiced in the quiet obedience of daily living. It is a simplicity that does not detract from the depth of faith but rather enhances it, offering a clear pathway to walking closely with Jehovah. As Micah 6:8 succinctly puts it, what Jehovah requires of us is to "do justice, and to love kindness, and to walk humbly with your God"—a call to a life of simple, faithful steps.

CHAPTER 5 Can We Truly Walk with God?

The Possibility of Divine Communion: Myth or Reality?

The question of whether humans can truly walk with God is as ancient as the Scriptures themselves. It is a question that penetrates the heart of faith and challenges the very essence of what believers hold to be true. Can finite beings really have communion with the Infinite? Is divine communion a myth, a spiritual ideal unattainable in reality, or is it the most profound truth accessible to the human soul?

The Biblical Affirmation of Walking with God

The Bible provides a resounding affirmation that walking with God is not a myth but a tangible reality. The Scriptural narratives depict various individuals who experienced profound communion with God. Enoch "walked with God, and he was not, for God took him" (Genesis 5:24), an enigmatic yet powerful testament to the depth of fellowship possible between the divine and the human. Noah was another who "walked with God" (Genesis 6:9), his life a beacon of righteousness in a corrupt age, marked by a closeness to Jehovah that saved him and his family from the deluge.

The Reality of Divine Encounter

These ancient accounts are not mere fables; they are rooted in the reality of divine encounter. Take Moses, for instance, who spoke with Jehovah as one speaks to a friend (Exodus 33:11). His interactions with Jehovah at the burning bush, on Mount Sinai, and throughout the wilderness journey showcase a relationship of both reverence and intimacy.

The Embodiment of Communion in Christ

The incarnation of Jesus Christ is the embodiment of divine communion, illustrating in the flesh what it means to walk with God. Jesus, in His very person, bridges the chasm between the divine and human, offering Himself as the way to the Father (John 14:6). His life and ministry are concrete examples of divine-human interaction, culminating in the cross where the ultimate expression of divine communion—reconciliation between God and man—is achieved.

The Witness of the Apostles

The apostles, those early followers of Christ, also lived lives of communion with God. Paul's conversion and subsequent relationship with God demonstrate the transformation that divine fellowship engenders. His epistles are saturated with the language of union with Christ and life in the Spirit, pointing to a lived experience that goes beyond mere doctrine.

The Experience of Believers Throughout History

Throughout history, believers have testified to the reality of walking with God. From the Desert Fathers and Mothers to contemporary testimonies, the narrative is consistent—communion with God is a lived experience that transforms lives. It is not the preserve of the mystic alone; it is the heritage of every believer.

The Role of the Holy Scriptures

While the idea of the Holy Spirit's indwelling is not a concept embraced in the conservative understanding, it is acknowledged that the Holy Scriptures serve as the conduit for divine communion. The Psalmist expresses, "Your word is a lamp to my feet and a light to my path" (Psalm 119:105), indicating the role of God's Word in guiding and nurturing a relationship with the divine.

The Dynamics of Prayer

Prayer is another vital aspect of this communion. It is the breath of the soul, the dialogue between the Creator and the creature. The Psalms offer a glimpse into the raw emotions of prayer—anger, joy, sorrow, and hope—all laid bare before Jehovah. They exemplify how prayer is not a monologue but a conversation, with the assurance that God listens and responds.

The Assurance of Divine Presence

The promise of divine presence assures believers that walking with God is not a distant dream but a present possibility. Jehovah's declaration "I will never leave you nor forsake you" (Hebrews 13:5), originally given to Joshua, reverberates through the ages to all who would draw near to God in faith.

The Evidence of Transformed Lives

The truest evidence of the possibility of divine communion is seen in transformed lives. Believers who once were bound by various vices are now living testimonies of the power of God to change hearts. The fruits of the Spirit—love, joy, peace, forbearance, kindness, goodness, faithfulness, gentleness, and self-control (Galatians 5:22-23)—are visible manifestations of a life walking in fellowship with God.

The Expectation of Eternal Communion

Finally, the expectation of eternal communion underscores the present reality of walking with God. Revelation speaks of a future where God will dwell with His people, wiping away every tear from their eyes (Revelation 21:3-4). The anticipation of this ultimate communion inspires believers to seek closeness with God here and now.

In sum, the question of whether we can walk with God finds its answer in the affirmative through the testimony of Scripture, the incarnation of Christ, the witness of the apostles, the experience of countless believers, and the transformative power evident in the lives of those who have dared to take God at His word. Divine communion is not a myth; it is the lifeblood of faith, a sacred reality woven into the fabric of Christian living. It is in this walking with God that one finds the purpose, meaning, and direction that our souls so earnestly crave.

Within Reach: The Attainable Walk with the Almighty

Walking with the Almighty is a concept woven throughout the tapestry of Scripture, embodying the closeness and personal nature of the relationship between the divine and humanity. This walk is not reserved for the spiritual elite or the heroes of faith whose stories sparkle on the pages of the Bible; it is an accessible path for every believer who seeks to align their life with God's will and purpose.

The Walk Defined

The walk with God is not a literal physical walk, but rather a metaphorical journey. It represents a lifestyle characterized by a consistent, conscious effort to align one's thoughts, actions, and decisions with the character and teachings of Jehovah. It's about the day-to-day choices that reflect a commitment to godliness and a rejection of the paths that lead away from God's righteousness.

The Biblical Paradigm

The Scriptures offer a plethora of examples regarding what this walk looks like in a tangible sense. Abraham, the father of faith, is summoned to leave his country and kindred to go to a land that Jehovah would show him (Genesis 12:1). His walk was not only physical but spiritual, stepping into the unknown, trusting in God's promises.

The Nature of Obedience

Obedience is a cornerstone of walking with God. It's a concept that requires a surrender of personal autonomy to the divine will. Consider the life of Joseph, who, despite being sold into slavery and unjustly imprisoned, maintained his integrity and obedience to God. His life was a testament to the principle that one's circumstances do not have to dictate one's spiritual state or commitment.

The Prophets' Call to Justice

The prophets, too, walked with Jehovah, delivering messages that were often unpopular but rooted in divine truth. They demonstrated that walking with God sometimes means standing alone, speaking against the tide of societal injustice and moral decay. Their walk was characterized by a bold proclamation of God's standards for his people.

The Simplicity of Devotion

Walking with Jehovah does not demand extraordinary acts but rather a simple, devoted heart. The Scriptures remind us that Jehovah does not look at the outward appearance but at the heart (1 Samuel 16:7). It is a heart that seeks to please God that finds the strength to walk in His ways.

The Encouragement of Fellowship

The walk with Jehovah is also encouraged by fellowship with other believers. The early church in the book of Acts exemplifies a community that walked together in the teachings of the apostles, in breaking of bread, and in prayers (Acts 2:42). It underscores that walking with God is not a solitary endeavor but one that is supported by the collective encouragement and accountability of the faith community.

The Test of Faith

The walk is not without its challenges. It's a journey that will test one's faith, as seen in the life of Job. His suffering was profound, yet his walk remained steadfast, showcasing that trials and tribulations do not negate the presence or the faithfulness of Jehovah but can deepen one's reliance on Him.

The Relevance of the Word

The Scriptures play a crucial role in this walk. They are the roadmap, providing guidance, comfort, and correction. Just as a lamp illuminates the path in darkness, so does God's Word light the way for those who walk with Him (Psalm 119:105). It informs, shapes, and guides the believer's steps.

The Pursuit of Wisdom

Wisdom is another vital aspect of walking with Jehovah. It is the practical application of knowledge and understanding in daily life. The book of Proverbs is replete with wisdom that is pertinent to walking in a manner that honors God, dealing with matters of speech, integrity, work ethic, and interpersonal relationships.

The Place of Humility

Humility is an essential attire for the walk. It is recognizing one's dependence on Jehovah, acknowledging human limitations, and submitting to God's sovereignty. The prophet Micah captures the essence of this walk when he asks, "What does Jehovah require of you but to do justice, to love kindness, and to walk humbly with your God?" (Micah 6:8).

The Commitment to Personal Holiness

Walking with Jehovah is a commitment to personal holiness. It's a continuous process of being set apart for God, resisting the pull of the world, and pursuing purity in thought and deed. Paul exhorts believers to walk in a manner worthy of the calling with which they have been called (Ephesians 4:1).

The Hope of Completion

Finally, the walk with Jehovah is one of hope and assurance that He who began a good work in believers will carry it on to completion until the day of Christ Jesus (Philippians 1:6). The walk may have its ebbs and flows, its mountains and valleys, but the destination is secured by the faithfulness of Jehovah.

In conclusion, the walk with the Almighty is not an elusive spiritual concept, but an attainable, concrete reality. It's the daily endeavor to live in a way that honors and pleases Jehovah, guided by His Word, empowered by His spirit, and supported by His people. It's a walk that is as real today as it was for the ancients who walked by faith, not by sight. Each step taken in faith is a step closer to fulfilling God's purpose for one's life.

CHAPTER 6 Will You Choose to Walk with God?

At the Crossroads of Will: Choosing the Path of Faith

Every individual stands at the crossroads of will at various junctures in life, moments when the direction of their spiritual journey is determined by the choices they make. The path of faith is one such direction, a road less traveled, requiring a conscious decision to walk in alignment with the teachings and precepts of Jehovah. This chapter examines the gravity of these decisions and the impact they have on one's relationship with God.

The Decision of Faith Is Personal

Choosing to walk with God is inherently a personal decision. It is not inherited or gained by association but made in the quiet recesses of one's heart. The story of Ruth, a Moabite woman, illustrates this beautifully. Despite her foreign background and the death of her Hebrew husband, she chose to cleave to Naomi and to Jehovah, declaring, "Your people will be my people and your God my God" (Ruth 1:16). Her choice was voluntary, personal, and transformative.

The Challenge of Choice

Choice by its nature implies the presence of alternatives. In the realm of faith, this often translates to the pull between God's way and the way of the world. Elijah presented such a choice to the Israelites on Mount Carmel, challenging them to decide between Jehovah and Baal (1 Kings 18:21). Today's believer faces similar choices, not on a mountain perhaps, but in the daily circumstances of life where choosing God's way requires intentional rejection of the contrary.

The Role of the Heart

In the Scriptures, the heart is often symbolic of one's inner life and inclinations. The condition of the heart greatly influences the choice to walk with God. King David is an example of a man after God's own heart (Acts 13:22), not because he was without fault, but because his heart was inclined towards Jehovah, prompting him to make choices that reflected repentance and a desire for divine fellowship.

The Power of the Will

The human will is a powerful faculty given by Jehovah. It is the ability to choose that reflects God's image in humans. The Bible does not advocate for a fatalistic approach to faith but rather presents the will as an active participant in the journey of faith. Joshua's declaration to the Israelites, "Choose for yourselves this day whom you will serve" (Joshua 24:15), underscores the active role of the will in spiritual commitment.

The Influence of the Mind

A decision for God is not made in a vacuum but is often a battle of the mind where truth contends with falsehood. The Apostle Paul knew this when he exhorted believers to be transformed by the renewing of their minds (Romans 12:2). A renewed mind equipped with scriptural truth is essential for making choices that are in harmony with God's will.

The Cost of Discipleship

Choosing the path of faith is also to acknowledge the cost of discipleship. Jesus himself spoke of counting the cost, of carrying one's cross daily to follow Him (Luke 14:27-28). The choice to walk with God is not a call to a trouble-free life but to a life of purpose and, sometimes, sacrifice.

The Impact of Environment

Environment and associations can influence the choices one makes about their walk with God. Daniel's resolve not to defile himself with the king's food (Daniel 1:8) is indicative of the proactive choices required to maintain one's walk in a potentially corrupting environment.

The Consistency of Choice

Walking with Jehovah is not a one-time choice but a series of daily decisions. Just as Israel had to collect manna each day, believers must daily choose to seek and follow God's guidance. The daily prayer of the psalmist, "Teach me your way, O Jehovah" (Psalm 27:11), captures the essence of this ongoing choice.

The Assurance of Divine Aid

While the decision to walk with God rests with the individual, it is not made without divine assistance. Jehovah's spirit acts as a helper, illuminating the mind and strengthening the will. This is not to suggest an indwelling in the charismatic sense, but a recognition of how God's word and providence work to guide and sustain the believer in their choices.

The Promise of Reward

Finally, the Scriptures offer a promise of reward for those who choose to walk with Jehovah. The book of Revelation speaks of a new heaven and a new earth for those who overcome (Revelation 21:1-7). It is the ultimate fruition of a walk begun in faith, sustained by choice, and completed in glory.

In essence, choosing to walk with Jehovah at the crossroads of will is a testament to the power and significance of free will in the divine-human relationship. It is an invitation to engage in the most consequential pursuit known to man: the pursuit of a faithful and purposeful life under the lordship of Jehovah. This choice is not a momentary declaration but a lifetime of deliberate and prayerful decisions that align with God's sovereign purpose, ultimately leading to a destiny that fulfills His creative intent for humanity.

Decision's Journey: The Choice to Walk with the Creator

The journey to walk with the Creator is not merely a single step but a continuous expedition filled with decisions that affirm our dedication and devotion to God. It is a journey marked by an evolving relationship with Jehovah, with each step reflecting a decision to know Him, trust Him, and act upon His Word.

The Choice to Begin

The initial choice to walk with Jehovah is a pivotal moment in the life of a believer. It is akin to Abram's call, where Jehovah said to him, "Go from your country, your people and your father's household to the land I will show you" (Genesis 12:1). Abram had to make a decisive choice to leave everything familiar and venture into the unknown because he trusted in God's promise. This is an illustration of the faith required to start the journey with Jehovah—a faith that is willing to trust in His promises even when the path ahead is not fully revealed.

The Process of Knowing God

To walk with the Creator, one must seek to know Him. The Scriptures are replete with the knowledge of God, and through them, one learns about His attributes, His will, and His purpose for humanity. David's meditations on the law of Jehovah day and night (Psalm 1:2) demonstrate the commitment to knowing God. It is through such meditation on God's word that one grows in understanding and becomes equipped for every good work (2 Timothy 3:16-17).

The Step of Trust

Walking with the Creator requires trust—a surrender of one's ways to God's ways. The Proverbs teach us to trust in Jehovah with all our heart and not to rely on our own understanding (Proverbs 3:5). Such trust is exemplified in the life of Joseph, who, despite being sold into slavery and unjustly imprisoned, trusted God's sovereignty and experienced God's providential care and ultimate redemption of his circumstances.

The Action of Obedience

The decision to walk with God is authenticated by obedience. It is one thing to profess faith, but it is another to live it out. Jesus said, "If you love me, keep my commands" (John 14:15). This love is not a mere feeling but is expressed in action—actions that reflect God's commandments and principles. Obedience is the tangible expression of faith, exemplified by Noah, who acted on God's warning and built the ark (Hebrews 11:7).

The Choice to Repent

Repentance is an integral part of the decision to walk with Jehovah. It involves a heartfelt sorrow for sin and a turning away from wrongdoing to embrace the ways of God. The story of King Manasseh, who turned from his wicked ways after being taken captive, demonstrates the power of repentance in restoring one's walk with Jehovah (2 Chronicles 33:12-13).

The Commitment to Persevere

The journey with the Creator is marked by perseverance. The writer of Hebrews encourages believers to run with perseverance the race marked out for them, fixing their eyes on Jesus (Hebrews 12:1-2). This perseverance is crucial, as the path is often fraught with trials and tribulations that test one's faith. Job's unwavering faith amidst profound suffering is a testament to the perseverance required to walk with God.

The Walk of Humility

Walking with God requires humility, a recognition of our dependency on Jehovah. It is understanding that "God opposes the proud but shows favor to the humble" (James 4:6). Moses was described as very humble, more than any man on the face of the earth (Numbers 12:3), which was pivotal for him to lead Israel and walk closely with Jehovah.

The Reflection of God's Character

As one walks with the Creator, there should be a transformation into His likeness. Paul speaks of being transformed into the same image from glory to glory (2 Corinthians 3:18). This transformation is a gradual process of character refinement, where traits such as love, joy, peace, patience, kindness, goodness, faithfulness, gentleness, and self-control become more evident in the believer's life (Galatians 5:22-23).

The Pursuit of Wisdom

Wisdom is fundamental in the choice to walk with Jehovah. It involves the application of God's principles in practical ways. King Solomon asked for wisdom to govern God's people, and it was granted to him (1 Kings 3:9-12). A believer must similarly pursue wisdom to navigate life's complexities in a way that honors Jehovah.

The Anticipation of God's Kingdom

The decision to walk with Jehovah is fueled by the anticipation of God's Kingdom. This hope is not a passive waiting but an active living out of principles that reflect the future reality of God's righteous rule. Jesus taught His disciples to seek first the Kingdom of God (Matthew 6:33), which means prioritizing God's righteousness in all decisions.

The Unwavering Focus on God's Purpose

To choose to walk with Jehovah is to align one's life with God's purpose. Paul's life after his conversion was characterized by a single-minded focus on the purpose to which he was called (Philippians 3:13-14). Similarly, believers are called to live a life worthy of the calling they have received (Ephesians 4:1), continually choosing God's purpose over personal ambition.

In conclusion, the decision to walk with the Creator is a multifaceted journey that entails beginning with faith, growing in the knowledge of God, trusting in His sovereignty, obeying His commandments, repenting from sin, persevering through trials, embracing humility, reflecting God's character, pursuing wisdom, anticipating His Kingdom, and focusing on His purpose. It is a journey that is attainable, personal, and transformational—a journey that brings one into intimate fellowship with Jehovah and aligns one's life with His eternal purposes.

CHAPTER 7 Walk with God Even in Times of Difficulty

Through Valleys and Shadows: Perseverance in Faith

In the walk with God, there will be times when the path leads through valleys and shadows, where the light seems dim, and the journey arduous. This is not a detour from the divine plan but an integral part of the spiritual terrain in a fallen world. God did not design suffering and difficulty as the tools of choice for our growth or to build character; instead, these experiences come as a consequence of a world marred by sin and rebellion against divine sovereignty. They serve as stark reminders of the inadequacy of human independence and the crucial need for divine guidance.

The Purpose of Perseverance

Perseverance in faith is the steadfast continuation on this path despite challenges. It is not merely endurance for endurance's sake; it is an active, purposeful assertion that Jehovah's ways are superior to our own, especially when the pressures of life threaten to dishearten us. Perseverance is not born out of an inherent strength of character but out of a reliance on Jehovah, who provides the strength necessary to endure.

The Nature of Human Suffering

Human suffering is an element of the broader object lesson that humanity is undergoing, an object lesson that highlights the repercussions of living apart from God's sovereignty. The Scriptures illustrate that trials will come, not as a celestial curriculum designed by God to teach us, but as the natural outcome of the human condition in a world that has strayed from Jehovah's original purpose.

The Example of Job

Consider Job, a man whose faith was tested to extremes. His suffering was not sent as a lesson from Jehovah but was allowed to unfold. Job's story is a vivid reminder that even the most righteous are not exempt from hardship. Yet, Job's perseverance is not a testament to his strength but to his unyielding trust in the Creator, despite his circumstances and profound grief.

The Wisdom of the Psalms

The Psalms provide a blueprint for expressing our deepest emotions before Jehovah. They offer language for the believer's heart during times of difficulty, encapsulating the cries of the faithful as they navigate the valleys of their journey. The Psalmist often speaks of walking through the valley of the shadow of death, yet fearing no evil, for Jehovah is with him (Psalm 23:4). This poetic expression encapsulates the essence of faith-filled perseverance—God is with us in our darkest valleys.

The Teaching of Jesus on Trials

Jesus, in His earthly ministry, never promised an absence of trials to His followers. Instead, He prepared them for the reality of difficulties, assuring them that in Him, they would have peace. In the world, they would have tribulation, but they could take heart because He has overcome the world (John 16:33). Here, Jesus lays out the foundation for perseverance: peace in Him, despite the turmoil without.

The Apostles' Perspective on Difficulties

The apostles echoed this theme in their letters to the early churches, recognizing the difficulties believers faced. James encourages believers to consider it pure joy when they face trials of many kinds because the testing of their faith produces perseverance (James 1:2-3). This is not a joy for the trial itself but a joy for the result of steadfast faith—a mature and complete faith that lacks nothing.

The Unseen Battle

Believers are reminded that they wrestle not against flesh and blood but against spiritual forces (Ephesians 6:12). The difficulties encountered are often more than mere physical or emotional battles; they are spiritual. Perseverance in faith, then, is also maintaining one's spiritual integrity and trust in Jehovah amidst these unseen battles.

The Role of Prayer in Perseverance

Prayer is the believer's lifeline to Jehovah, especially in times of trouble. It is through prayer that believers maintain their connection with God, express their dependence on Him, and draw on the strength that He provides. The fervent prayers of a righteous person have great power (James 5:16), not because of the person's righteousness but because of the One to whom they are praying.

The Comfort of the Holy Scriptures

The Holy Scriptures are a source of comfort and guidance through the difficult times. They remind the believer of God's faithfulness in the past, provide wisdom for the present, and hope for the future. Paul writes that everything that was written in the past was written to teach us, so that through endurance and the encouragement of the Scriptures we might have hope (Romans 15:4).

The Endurance of Hope

Hope is an anchor for the soul, firm and secure (Hebrews 6:19). It is this hope that sustains believers through the trials. This hope is not wishful thinking but a confident expectation based on the promises of God, who cannot lie. It is this hope that undergirds perseverance, ensuring that even in the darkest valleys, the believer can look forward to the fulfillment of Jehovah's promises.

To persevere in faith through valleys and shadows is to cling to Jehovah's promise of His unchanging presence and to trust in His sovereign purposes, even when those purposes are obscured by the trials of life. It is to walk humbly with our God, not only in times of joy and peace but also in times of difficulty and distress. This perseverance is not a grim march but a hopeful, steady progression toward the ultimate realization of God's purpose for humanity—to walk with Him in righteousness and peace, free from the shadows and valleys of this present world.

Resilient Steps: The Walk of Faith Amidst Life's Storms

In the spiritual odyssey of a believer, resilience is the buoyant force that allows one to navigate the tempestuous seas of life. The walk of faith is not a promenade along serene shores; it often leads through tumultuous storms. These seasons of distress, however, are instrumental in redirecting our gaze from self-reliance to the unassailable sovereignty of Jehovah.

Understanding Divine Allowance

The acknowledgment that Jehovah does not orchestrate suffering for growth but allows it within His sovereign domain is critical. It underlines the fact that suffering, while existent, is not divinely desired. The heart of the Creator is not for humanity to endure pain, but in His omniscience, He permits it, knowing it can lead to a deeper awareness of our need for Him. Life's storms are not punishments but permitted challenges that expose our fragility and the futility of human independence.

The Legacy of the Faithful

The biblical narrative is rich with exemplars who walked faithfully amidst life's storms. David, the shepherd turned king, penned psalms that resonate with the very essence of resilience. From his anointing to his ascension to the throne, his life was punctuated with peril. Yet, in his wanderings and woes, David's faith was not quenched but kindled. He danced before Jehovah with all his might, even when scorned (2

Samuel 6:14-16). His resilience was not in his royalty but in his relentless pursuit of God's heart.

The Steadfastness of Paul

Paul the Apostle embodies the walk of faith amidst adversity. Shipwrecked, beaten, and imprisoned, Paul's journey was fraught with adversities that would have crippled the faith of many. Nevertheless, his letters bear the hallmark of joy and hope. *"For our light affliction, which is but for a moment, worketh for us a far more exceeding and eternal weight of glory,"* he wrote to the Corinthians (2 Corinthians 4:17). This perspective reflects a resilient step—a stride that looks beyond the present storm to the eternal calm.

Embracing the Lesson

The inherent flaw in human independence is starkly evident when the storms of life rage. It is here that the object lesson is most profoundly learned. Humanity's detachment from divine sovereignty is a self-inflicted exile into chaos. Suffering then becomes a backdrop against which the sovereignty of God is starkly contrasted with human inadequacy. The storm itself is not the teacher; it is in the seeking of shelter that the lesson is learned.

The Comfort in Christ's Suffering

In the suffering of Christ, there is an unmatched solace for believers. The Messiah did not remain aloof from the afflictions of mortality. *"Surely he hath borne our griefs, and carried our sorrows,"* prophesied Isaiah (Isaiah 53:4). In Jesus' suffering, there is a companionship in sorrow and a model for resilience. He faced the ultimate storm not as a display of divine stoicism but as the epitome of faithful endurance.

The Assurance of God's Presence

The quintessential comfort in any storm is the assurance of Jehovah's presence. *"I will never leave thee, nor forsake thee,"* Jehovah promises (Hebrews 13:5). This is the foundation upon which resilience is built—the unshakeable knowledge that one does not walk alone. The tempest may howl, and the waves may roar, but the believer treads each waterlogged step with the confidence that the Creator Himself is the companion.

Navigating Storms with the Word

The Scriptures serve as the compass and chart for navigating life's gales. They do not offer a detour around the storm but provide the guidance to pass through it. The Word of God is replete with assurances, principles, and precepts that anchor the soul. It is a source of illumination in the obscurity that storms often bring.

The Ministry of the Comforter

Even though there is no indwelling of the Holy Spirit, the Spirit of God is active in ministry and comfort. As Jesus comforted His disciples with the promise of the Spirit who would be with them, so believers today can take solace in the fact that the Scriptures and the example of Christ serve as a continuous source of solace and strength provided by God.

The Fellowship of Suffering

There is a communal aspect to the walk of faith amidst storms. Believers are called to bear one another's burdens (Galatians 6:2), to weep with those who weep, and to provide a shoulder for the weary. The resilience of faith is fortified in the community of the faithful, where encouragement and support are abundantly available.

The Testimony in Trials

In the crucible of trials, the believer's faith is refined and becomes a testimony to others. As a lighthouse stands firm amidst the onslaught of the sea, so a resilient faith serves as a beacon to those lost in the tempest of life. The believer's perseverance proclaims the faithfulness of Jehovah, even when words are insufficient.

The resilient steps in the walk of faith amidst life's storms are thus marked by a deep-seated trust in Jehovah's sovereignty and an unwavering focus on His promises. As the psalmist declared, *"Though I walk through the valley of the shadow of death, I will fear no evil: for thou art with me"* (Psalm 23:4), so the believer walks, not in denial of the storms but in defiance of despair, with eyes fixed on the Creator, whose purpose and presence are the ultimate haven from life's fiercest gales.

CHAPTER 8 Carry on in Your Walking with God

Enduring the Marathon: Longevity in Your Spiritual Walk

To walk with God is to embark on a journey not of sprinting speed but of marathon endurance. The Christian life is frequently depicted in Scripture not as a brief dash to victory but as a long-distance race requiring stamina, patience, and unwavering dedication. This spiritual marathon is one marked by persistent faithfulness, where the true measure of success is not in the swiftness of our stride but in the steadfastness of our steps.

The Principle of Persistence

Longevity in our spiritual walk with Jehovah hinges on the principle of persistence. Persistence is the quiet resolve that presses us forward when the thrill of the start has faded and the finish line is nowhere in sight. It is the determined effort to maintain a steady pace in our relationship with God, even when the initial zeal may wane. It's exemplified in the life of Noah, who, for decades, remained faithful to God's command to build the ark amid a world that was oblivious to the coming judgment (Genesis 6:22). His persistent obedience was not a mere moment of faith but a prolonged demonstration of unwavering commitment to God's direction.

Cultivating Consistency

Consistency in our walk with God is crucial to endurance. It's about establishing regular patterns of worship, prayer, and Scripture study. It is in the daily devotion, the consistent turning of our hearts towards Jehovah, that we find the strength to continue. The Psalms frequently affirm the necessity of daily seeking God: *"O God, thou art my God; early will I seek thee"* (Psalm 63:1). This daily rhythm becomes the heartbeat of a walk that endures through all seasons.

Learning from the Patriarchs

The patriarchs — Abraham, Isaac, and Jacob — offer concrete examples of enduring faith. They each faced varied trials and decades of waiting on Jehovah's promises. Abraham waited 25 years for the fulfillment of Jehovah's promise of a son (Genesis 21:5). Throughout these long years, he stumbled at times, yet he is commended for his faith in Jehovah, who "calls into existence the things that do not exist" (Romans 4:17). This longevity in faith was not due to Abraham's personal strength but to his anchored trust in the One who is faithful.

Embracing Spiritual Disciplines

To ensure longevity in our spiritual walk, embracing spiritual disciplines is essential. These practices are not mere religious duties but are the means by which we align our hearts with God's will. Prayer, fasting, service, and meditation on God's Word are not checkboxes for spiritual accomplishment but avenues for sustaining our spiritual vitality. They are the spiritual nourishment for the marathon runner's soul.

Facing Trials with Tenacity

The biblical account of Job provides a powerful template for tenacity. Job's life was struck by calamity, yet he clung to his integrity and his God, despite not understanding the reasons for his suffering. His endurance was not a stoic resignation but a robust clinging to the reality of God's ultimate justice and goodness. He declared, *"Though he slay me, yet will I trust in him"* (Job 13:15), exemplifying an endurance that rests not on the absence of adversity but on the character of Jehovah.

The Promise of Renewal

In the marathon of faith, there is the divine promise of renewal for those who might grow weary. *"They that wait upon Jehovah shall renew their strength; they shall mount up with wings as eagles; they shall run, and not be weary; and they shall walk, and not faint"* (Isaiah 40:31). This assurance provides a second wind to the fatigued and encouragement to the disheartened. It is Jehovah Himself who revitalizes our spirit and rejuvenates our resolve to continue in our walk with Him.

The Witness of the Early Church

The early church, as chronicled in the Acts of the Apostles, presents a vibrant illustration of enduring commitment. Faced with persecution and internal challenges, the early Christians persisted in their proclamation of the Gospel and their communal fellowship. Their endurance was rooted not in their numbers or their resources but in their collective reliance on Jehovah's spirit and guidance.

Mentorship and Accountability

In the realm of endurance, mentorship and accountability play a pivotal role. Paul's relationship with Timothy is illustrative of this dynamic. Paul's letters to Timothy are rich with exhortation and encouragement, urging him to perseverance in faith and ministry. Spiritual mentorship provides guidance and wisdom, while accountability offers support and encouragement, both critical for the long haul.

The Hope of the Prize

Finally, the motivation for endurance in our spiritual marathon is the hope of the prize that lies ahead. Paul spoke of pressing towards the goal for the prize of the upward call of God in Christ Jesus (Philippians 3:14). This eternal perspective fuels our endurance, giving purpose to our every step and driving us to carry on in our walk with God.

The Christian marathon is not won by swift sprints or momentary bursts of enthusiasm but by the steady, resolute, and continual placing of one foot in front of the other. It is the cumulative steps taken in faith, the persistent pursuit of God's presence, and the relentless reliance on His promises that mark a walk of longevity. As we journey through this marathon, may we do so with our eyes firmly set on Jehovah, "the author and finisher of our faith" (Hebrews 12:2), who provides both the strength and the destination for our spiritual walk.

Unwavering Progress: Continuing Your Path with God

In the journey of faith, unwavering progress is not marked by leaps and bounds, but rather by the constant, often imperceptible movement closer to the heart of Jehovah. The path we walk with God is rarely a straight line; it meanders through mountains and valleys, yet it always presses forward.

The Vitality of Steadfastness

Steadfastness is the lifeblood of unwavering progress in our walk with God. It is the spiritual fortitude that undergirds our steps when the path grows dim and our destination seems distant. Just as the oak tree grows slowly, almost imperceptibly, but stands strong for centuries, so must our spiritual growth be marked by enduring faithfulness. In the book of James, believers are encouraged to let steadfastness have its full effect, that they may be *"perfect and complete, lacking in nothing"* (James 1:4). This maturity in faith comes not from transient experiences but from the deep roots of unshakeable trust in Jehovah.

The Journey of Abraham

Consider Abraham's journey: from Ur to Haran, from Haran to Canaan, from Canaan to Egypt, and back to Canaan again. His path was not straightforward. He experienced famine, conflict, and even his own failings. Yet, he progressed in his relationship with Jehovah, learning to rely more fully on God's promises with each step. His life was a testament to unwavering progress, not because he never faltered, but because he never ceased to get back up and continue his walk with God.

Maintaining a Heart for God

King David's life offers an illustration of maintaining a heart for God amidst personal failure and societal pressures. Though he was anointed as a young shepherd boy, David's path to the throne was fraught with peril. Even after assuming the throne, his journey with Jehovah encountered the valleys of moral failure and family turmoil. Yet, David's heart, described as *"after God's own heart,"* continued to seek Jehovah's presence earnestly, expressing itself in psalms that ranged from lament to exuberant praise. His progress is seen in his ongoing repentance and renewed commitment to Jehovah's ways.

The Discipline of Daily Communion

Daily communion with Jehovah through prayer, worship, and Scripture meditation is the discipline that keeps us on the path. It's the daily bread for our souls, sustaining us through every season. The prophet Daniel exemplifies this daily discipline. Even in the face of a decree that could have cost him his life, Daniel continued to pray three times a day, just as he had done before (Daniel 6:10). His communion with Jehovah was not casual or intermittent; it was a lifeline that held firm even when the lions' den loomed before him.

The Metaphor of Walking

The metaphor of walking is apt for our faith journey. Walking is a series of steps, a continuous motion that propels us forward. The Christian life is much like walking; each step may seem small, but over time, the distance covered can be vast. The apostle Paul exhorted the church in Colossians to *"walk in a manner worthy of the Lord, fully pleasing to him"* (Colossians 1:10). It's a daily endeavor, full of small decisions and moments that, together, shape the trajectory of our spiritual journey.

The Resolve of Nehemiah

Nehemiah's resolve in rebuilding the walls of Jerusalem, despite opposition and distraction, reflects the essence of unwavering progress. He did not allow the scorn of Sanballat and Tobiah to deter him from the task Jehovah had set before him (Nehemiah 4:1-3). Instead, he responded with prayer and persistence, keeping his focus on the work at hand. Nehemiah's progress was marked by prayerful action and an unyielding commitment to the completion of God's work.

Continuity in Change

Our path with God is characterized by continuity in change. As the Israelites followed the cloud by day and the fire by night in the wilderness, they remained in continuous motion toward the Promised Land, even as their surroundings constantly changed (Exodus 13:21-22). Our own journey may lead us through changing circumstances, but the goal remains constant: a deeper communion with Jehovah, a life reflecting His character and purposes.

The Example of Paul

The apostle Paul's life was a vivid display of unwavering progress. From a zealous persecutor of the church to one of its most prolific apostles, Paul's journey with Christ was dynamic and challenging. Despite beatings, shipwrecks, imprisonments, and constant danger, Paul pressed on, his eyes fixed not on his struggles but on the prize of his high calling in Christ Jesus (Philippians 3:14). His endurance wasn't rooted in personal ambition but in his unwavering commitment to the Gospel and his unrelenting progress towards God's purposes.

In sum, unwavering progress in our walk with God is the steady advance of a heart firmly planted in the soil of faith, drawing nourishment from daily communion with Jehovah and remaining resolute in the face of life's vicissitudes. It is to walk hand in hand with God through the tapestry of life's experiences, always forward, always upward, keeping in step with the Spirit's lead, as we carry on toward eternity with God.

CHAPTER 9 Continuously Walking in the Truth

Without Cease: The Constant Walk in God's Reality

The life of a Christian is not a series of spiritual sprints; it is a marathon of faithfulness where the follower of Christ is called to walk without cease in the reality of God's truth. It is in the constancy of this walk that believers demonstrate their commitment to God's purpose for their lives, reflecting His truth in every aspect of their existence.

The Continuity of Enoch's Walk with God

Enoch's life offers an extraordinary example of continuous walking in truth. Scripture succinctly states that *"Enoch walked with God; and he was not, for God took him"* (Genesis 5:24). Enoch's walk was so aligned with God's will that he was translated directly to be with Jehovah. This profound union with God was not the result of an occasional meeting with the Divine but a persistent, daily walk—a lifestyle of communion with Jehovah.

The Constant Communion of Prayer

Prayer is the communication channel through which we walk in God's reality. It is the breath of the soul, the secret place of the Most High where the believer speaks and listens to Jehovah. Daniel, as mentioned previously, maintained his communion with God through prayer, despite the edicts of kings and the threat of lions. The disciples, following Jesus' ascension, *"all joined together constantly in prayer"* (Acts 1:14), laying the foundation for the early church in uninterrupted communion with Jehovah.

The Undeviating Pursuit of Truth

Walking without cease in God's reality involves an undeviating pursuit of truth as revealed in the Scriptures. The Bereans were commended because they *"received the word with all eagerness, examining the Scriptures daily to see if these things were so"* (Acts 17:11). They did not casually approach God's word, nor did they rest on the laurels of past understandings. They sought Jehovah's truth continually, allowing it to shape their reality each day.

The Faithful Endurance of Job

Job's steadfastness in the midst of suffering encapsulates a life lived in the unrelenting reality of God's sovereignty. He did not understand all the reasons behind his sufferings, yet he refused to curse God. Instead, he persistently sought Jehovah's presence and purpose. His walk in God's reality was unwavering, even when that reality was shrouded in pain and mystery. *"Though he slay me, yet will I hope in him,"* Job declared (Job 13:15), anchoring his walk in the unchangeable character of God.

The Unchanging Character of God

Walking in God's reality demands recognition of His unchanging character. Jehovah is the same *"yesterday and today and forever"* (Hebrews 13:8). Our walk with God must be built on the bedrock of His eternal nature and His revealed Word, not the shifting sands of human philosophy or fleeting cultural norms. Just as a house built on a solid foundation withstands the storms, so too does a life grounded in the immutable truth of Jehovah endure the vicissitudes of life.

The Perseverance of Paul

Paul's perseverance illustrates a constant walk in God's reality amidst adversity. His epistles are replete with encouragements to continue steadfastly in the faith, such as when he exhorts believers to *"stand firm in the Lord"* (Philippians 4:1). His own life was an exemplar of this endurance, as he faced hardships and persecution with a focus not on the temporary trials but on the eternal glory that far outweighs them.

The Integration of Truth into Life

Walking in God's reality is not merely a cognitive assent to doctrinal truths; it is the integration of these truths into the fabric of daily life. The wisdom literature of Proverbs teaches that *"in all your ways acknowledge him, and he will make straight your paths"* (Proverbs 3:6). The constant walk with Jehovah encompasses decisions, relationships, work, and worship, infusing all with the fragrance of divine truth.

The Vitality of Spiritual Vigilance

Vigilance is crucial in our continuous walk. The enemy seeks to deceive and derail, but the vigilant believer, armed with the full armor of God, can stand against the schemes of the devil (Ephesians 6:11-17). Spiritual vigilance is not an intermittent effort; it is a constant guard, a continual watchfulness over one's heart and mind in Christ Jesus.

The Unbroken Communion

Therefore, to walk without cease in God's reality is to live with unbroken communion with Jehovah, to pray without ceasing, to pursue truth relentlessly, and to integrate God's eternal Word into every aspect of one's being. It is to acknowledge Jehovah's sovereignty even in suffering, to rest on His unchangeable character, to persevere in the faith despite adversity, and to remain vigilant against spiritual complacency or compromise. In this walk, believers reflect the life-transforming power of the gospel, a light that shines in the darkness, guiding their steps on the pathway to everlasting life with God. It is this unrelenting progress towards His purposes that we strive for as we journey through life's terrain, continuously walking in the truth that Jehovah has laid before us.

Perpetual Motion: Advancing in Truth Every Day

The journey of faith is not marked by idleness but by perpetual motion—an ongoing, daily advance in the truth of God's Word. This forward movement is the essence of spiritual growth, a continual stepping out in faith and obedience to the truths revealed in Scripture.

The Principle of Daily Renewal

In this pursuit of advancing in truth every day, the believer is called to a principle of daily renewal. *"Therefore we do not lose heart. Though outwardly we are wasting away, yet inwardly we are being renewed day by day"* (2 Corinthians 4:16). This inward renewal is a conscious, daily return to the wellspring of life found in God's Word, drawing fresh water for today's journey.

The Preeminence of God's Word

God's Word stands as the preeminent guide for this daily advance. As the psalmist declares, *"Your word is a lamp to my feet and a light to my path"* (Psalm 119:105), it is through the consistent engagement with Scripture that the path of truth is illuminated, guiding believers in every decision, action, and thought.

The Example of Daily Bread

Jesus' teaching on prayer includes the request for daily bread, a metaphor extending beyond the physical to encompass spiritual nourishment. Just as the body requires daily sustenance, so too does the soul require the daily bread of God's truth. It is not a feast intended for sporadic indulgence but a staple for daily consumption.

The Practice of Daily Obedience

Advancing in truth also requires the practice of daily obedience. It's in the seemingly small choices and acts of obedience that faith is lived out. Consider the detailed instructions given for the construction of the Tabernacle in Exodus. Each act of obedience in following Jehovah's specifications was an advance in living out His truth.

The Continuity of Abiding in Christ

Jesus spoke of the necessity of abiding in Him, *"I am the vine; you are the branches. Whoever abides in me and I in him, he it is that bears much fruit, for apart from me you can do nothing"* (John 15:5). Abiding is not a once-in-a-lifetime event but a continuous state. It is in this unbroken connection with Christ that a believer grows and advances in truth.

The Dynamics of Spiritual Discipline

The advancement in truth is fueled by spiritual discipline. Like a skilled artisan honing his craft day by day, the Christian must engage in the spiritual disciplines of prayer, study, meditation, and service continually. This is not legalism but a voluntary, joy-filled practice that aligns the heart with God's will.

The Incremental Progress of Sanctification

Sanctification, the process by which we are made holy, is inherently incremental. Paul reminds believers to *"work out your own salvation with fear and trembling"* (Philippians 2:12). This work is an ongoing process, a series of steps taken each day to grow in godliness and truth.

The Vitality of Perseverance

Perseverance is essential for daily advancement in truth. The epistle to the Hebrews encourages, *"Let us run with perseverance the race marked out for us"* (Hebrews 12:1). It is the daily, consistent running—persevering through trials, doubts, and hardships—that marks the true forward motion of the believer.

The Consistency of Hope

Hope provides the horizon for this daily journey. Anchored in the promises of God, hope propels the believer forward, offering the assurance of God's faithfulness. *"For in this hope we were saved. Now hope that is seen is not hope. For who hopes for what he sees?"* (Romans 8:24). It is this unseen hope that sustains the believer's daily walk in truth.

Conclusion: The Unending Ascent

Thus, the daily walk in truth is an unending ascent, a climb toward spiritual maturity. Each day is an opportunity to take up the cross, to live out the realities of God's kingdom here on earth, and to draw nearer to Jehovah. This ascent is neither rapid nor easy, but it is the path laid out for those who would follow Christ, who have committed to putting God's purpose first in their lives. In the perpetual motion of advancing in truth every day, believers are transformed, becoming more like Christ, ready to meet Jehovah with hearts shaped by His Word and lives that testify to His enduring truth.

CHAPTER 10 Examine Yourselves to See Whether You Are in the Faith

Self-Reflection: Testing the Authenticity of Faith

The earnest believer is no stranger to the internal examination of faith, a pivotal practice underscored by Paul when he writes, *"Examine yourselves, to see whether you are in the faith. Test yourselves"* (2 Corinthians 13:5). This self-reflection is not an occasional audit but a continuous self-scrutiny to authenticate the genuineness of one's faith.

The Foundation of Self-Examination

Self-reflection begins with a foundational understanding of faith's nature. Faith, according to Hebrews, is *"the assurance of things hoped for, the conviction of things not seen"* (Hebrews 11:1). Therefore, to test the authenticity of faith is to assess the substance of one's assurance and conviction in God's promises and character.

The Role of Scripture in Self-Examination

Scripture acts as the mirror in which faith is examined. James compares the Word of God to a mirror, stating that anyone who hears the Word but fails to act on it is like a man who looks at himself, goes away, and immediately forgets what he looks like (James 1:23-24). It is by looking intently into the perfect law that one can see their true spiritual reflection and make necessary adjustments.

The Personal Honesty Required

Testing the authenticity of faith requires brutal personal honesty. It demands acknowledgment of one's shortcomings and the humility to confess them before Jehovah. David's plea in Psalm 139:23-24, *"Search me, O God, and know my heart! Try me and know my thoughts!"* embodies the earnest desire for God to reveal any misgivings in one's heart.

The Evidence of Fruit Bearing

The evidence of a genuine faith is seen in the bearing of fruit. Jesus said, *"Every healthy tree bears good fruit, but the diseased tree bears bad fruit"* (Matthew 7:17). A self-examination involves looking at one's life to see if it bears the fruits of the Spirit, which are love, joy, peace, patience, kindness, goodness, faithfulness, gentleness, and self-control (Galatians 5:22-23).

The Importance of Prayer in Self-Reflection

Prayer is integral to self-reflection. It is the means by which a believer communicates with God, seeking enlightenment and strength to align more closely with His will. In prayer, one may ask for the discernment needed to see where their faith may waver and for the courage to fortify it.

The Significance of Obedience

Obedience is a clear indicator of faith's authenticity. The apostle John writes that keeping God's commandments is how we know that we know Him (1 John 2:3). Self-examination often reveals whether one's life is marked by an obedience that stems from faith or is tainted by lip service without corresponding actions.

The Witness of Conscience

Conscience serves as a witness in the trial of faith. A clear conscience is one outcome of a faith that is vibrant and authentic. Paul speaks of his own conscience bearing witness in the Holy Spirit that he has conducted himself with godly sincerity and grace (Romans 9:1). A believer's conscience, when informed and guided by Scripture, is a powerful tool for self-assessment.

The Reflection on Suffering

Reflection on how one navigates suffering and trials also tests the authenticity of faith. Trials come to prove our faith and produce steadfastness (James 1:2-4). The manner in which a believer responds to adversity is a strong indicator of the depth and reality of their faith.

The Practice of Repentance

An authentic faith is not devoid of sin, but it is characterized by a heart posture of repentance. John writes that if we say we have no sin, we deceive ourselves, and the truth is not in us. However, if we confess our sins, God is faithful to forgive us and cleanse us from all unrighteousness (1 John 1:8-9). Repentance is a continuous practice in the life of a faithful believer.

The Accountability to the Body of Christ

Self-reflection on one's faith does not occur in isolation but within the accountability of the body of Christ. The church acts as a community of faith where believers can encourage one another and help in the self-examination process, holding each other accountable to live out the truth of the gospel.

Conclusion: A Continuous Journey

Thus, the self-reflection on the authenticity of one's faith is not a one-time event but a continuous journey. It is an integral part of walking humbly with God, a deliberate and honest assessment of one's alignment with God's will, the depth of one's trust in His promises, and the consistency of one's obedience to His commands. As believers embark on this journey of self-examination, they are drawn into a closer communion with God, ensuring that His purpose is always at the forefront of their lives.

Faith Under Scrutiny: The Examination of Belief

The call to examine our faith is a clarion call from the Scriptures, echoing through the corridors of time to every believer's heart. This examination is a profound endeavor, not to be taken lightly, for it is in the crucible of scrutiny that the true mettle of belief is revealed and refined.

The Intent of Examination

The intent of examining our belief is not to induce self-doubt but to affirm the solidity and sincerity of our faith. It serves to reinforce our commitment to Jehovah and to ensure that our walk aligns with His divine precepts. The Psalmist captures this sentiment when he pleads with Jehovah to test him and try his heart (Psalm 26:2).

The Reflective Heart

The reflective heart is one that looks inward with the aid of God's Word, seeking to understand the nuances of its own belief. It's about probing deeply into our faith-life to see whether Christ truly lives within us. As Paul charges the Corinthians to test themselves, it's evident that the reflective heart is crucial in the life of a believer (2 Corinthians 13:5).

The Unchanging Standard

The unchanging standard by which we must examine our belief is the Word of God. It is the plumb line that sets our lives straight, the solid rock upon which we stand. Scripture holds up the mirror to our souls, revealing the truth about our spiritual condition. We must approach it not as a passive reader but as an active participant, allowing it to penetrate our hearts and minds (Hebrews 4:12).

Conviction Versus Comfort

Our belief is not measured by the comfort it provides but by the convictions it imparts. True faith can often lead us into uncomfortable truths about ourselves and the world around us. It calls for an unswerving allegiance to Jehovah's standards, even when such fidelity may attract opposition or bring us into conflict with the prevailing currents of our time.

The Evidence of a Transformed Life

The evidence of a transformed life stands as a testament to the authenticity of our belief. A faith that does not prompt change is like the dead faith spoken of in James 2:17. Transformation is the fruit of genuine belief, displayed in a life that continuously evolves to reflect Jehovah's character and will.

The Honesty in Prayer

Honesty in prayer is paramount when examining our belief. It is through prayer that we lay bare our souls before Jehovah, seeking His guidance and wisdom. In the quietude of prayer, we find the space to ask the difficult questions and to receive the strength to face the truths that emerge.

The Assessment of Obedience

The assessment of obedience is a key component in the examination of belief. Our fidelity to Jehovah's commands is the practical outworking of our faith. Obedience is the visible expression of our belief, revealing whether we are merely hearers of the Word or doers of it (James 1:22).

The Resilience Through Trials

Resilience through trials is another gauge of our belief. As gold is tested by fire, so our faith is tested by the tribulations we encounter (1 Peter 1:7). How we withstand these trials, how we maintain our trust in Jehovah amidst the tempest, speaks volumes about the depth and durability of our belief.

The Alignment With God's Will

Alignment with God's will is the ultimate goal of our faith examination. It's not enough to merely believe in Jehovah's existence; even the demons believe that much (James 2:19). Our belief must be synchronized with God's will, manifesting in a life devoted to serving His purposes above our own.

The Interpersonal Reflection

Interpersonal reflection on how our belief affects our relationships with others also provides a window into the state of our faith. We are told that the two greatest commandments revolve around love—for Jehovah and for our neighbors (Matthew 22:37-39). How we embody this love in our interactions is indicative of our belief's integrity.

The Perseverance in Doctrine

Perseverance in doctrine is critical when scrutinizing our belief. In an age of shifting values and relative truths, steadfastness in apostolic teaching is a hallmark of genuine faith. Paul emphasizes the importance of holding to the traditions and teachings passed on to the believers (2 Thessalonians 2:15).

The Community of Faith as a Mirror

The community of faith acts as a mirror, reflecting the collective belief and individual contributions to the body of Christ. Our interaction within this community—how we build one another up, hold each other accountable, and operate as one body—provides insights into the quality of our individual faith (1 Corinthians 12:27).

Conclusion: The Outcome of Examination

The outcome of a rigorous examination of belief should be a fortified, more vibrant faith. It is through this process that we are drawn into a closer relationship with Jehovah, assured of our place in His purpose, and equipped to walk humbly with our God. The process of examination is not about reaching perfection but about pursuing spiritual maturity, ensuring that our faith is not in vain but is a living, active force in every aspect of our lives.

CHAPTER 11 Walking with God in Spite of Doubt

Understanding Uncertainty: The Role of Doubt in Faith

Doubt, often perceived as a treacherous enemy of faith, is in reality a ubiquitous aspect of the human condition. In our walk with God, we are not immune to the waves of uncertainty that can suddenly arise and challenge the very foundations of our belief. Yet, it is crucial to understand that the presence of doubt does not signify the absence of faith; rather, it can act as a catalyst for growth, compelling us to seek deeper truths and reaffirm our commitment to Jehovah.

The Nature of Doubt

Doubt is not a modern phenomenon; it is as ancient as faith itself. Even the patriarch Abraham, when promised a son, questioned how it could be, considering his and Sarah's advanced age (Genesis 17:17). His doubt did not go unnoticed by Jehovah, nor did it ultimately disqualify him from being the father of nations. Doubt, in this sense, can be a natural response to the unfolding mysteries of God's promises and His workings in our lives.

The Duality of Doubt

Doubt possesses a duality—it can either lead to spiritual paralysis or propel us toward a more profound understanding of Jehovah's character and will. When the disciples of Jesus expressed their uncertainties, He did not cast them away; rather, He provided reassurance and evidence of His divine nature (John 20:27). It is in the grappling with doubt that one's faith is often fortified, emerging more resilient and enlightened.

Navigating the Seas of Uncertainty

Navigating the seas of uncertainty requires a compass, and that compass is the Word of God. It offers the illumination required to see through the fog of doubt. The psalmist proclaims God's Word as a lamp unto his feet and a light unto his path (Psalm 119:105), reminding us that even in moments of indecision, Jehovah provides the guidance necessary to continue our journey.

The Honesty of Doubt

The honesty of doubt is an essential aspect of a genuine relationship with Jehovah. When Job faced his immense suffering, he did not shy away from expressing his confusion and distress before God (Job 7:20). It is this candidness that Jehovah ultimately commends, not the feigned certainty of Job's friends who claimed to speak for God without truly understanding His ways.

The Process of Wrestling with Questions

The process of wrestling with questions can serve as a divine mechanism for refining our beliefs. It forces us to confront the depth of our convictions and to seek Jehovah in a manner that superficial faith cannot. When Jacob wrestled with the angel, he emerged with a new name, Israel, symbolizing his struggle with God and with humans and how he had overcome (Genesis 32:28). Similarly, our spiritual struggles can lead to a new identity and a stronger, more dynamic faith.

The Reinforcement of Conviction

The reinforcement of conviction in the face of doubt is a testament to the power of persistent faith. Thomas, one of the twelve apostles, is often remembered for his doubt. Yet, upon being presented with the evidence of Christ's resurrection, his proclamation of faith was unequivocal (John 20:28). His journey from doubt to faith underscores that certainty often comes through a period of questioning.

The Community of Believers

The community of believers plays a pivotal role in navigating doubt. Through the sharing of personal experiences, insights from Scripture, and mutual encouragement, the body of Christ acts as a support system for those wrestling with uncertainty. The New Testament church was marked by its fellowship and communal support, a practice that provided the early Christians with strength and reassurance (Acts 2:42-47).

Embracing the Mystery of God

Embracing the mystery of God is a humble acknowledgment that, as finite beings, there will always be facets of Jehovah's nature and plans that we cannot fully comprehend. The Apostle Paul speaks of seeing through a glass darkly, recognizing that our current understanding is partial and will only be made complete in Jehovah's due time (1 Corinthians 13:12).

The Fruitfulness of Perseverance

The fruitfulness of perseverance through doubt can lead to a more nuanced and mature faith. Just as a tree's roots grow deeper when searching for water during a drought, our spiritual roots delve deeper into Jehovah's truths when we seek Him amidst our doubts. The endurance of faith through these trials produces character and hope (Romans 5:3-4).

Conclusion: Doubt as a Companion on the Journey

In conclusion, doubt should be understood not as an antagonist to faith, but as a companion on the journey—a challenging companion, certainly, but one that can spur us to seek Jehovah with greater zeal. In "Walk Humbly with Your God: Putting God's Purpose First in Your Life," we acknowledge that a faith untested by doubt may remain shallow, while a faith that survives and thrives through doubt can reach profound depths. The role of doubt in faith is not to undermine, but to undergird—a foundation upon which a more resilient, authentic faith is built. As we walk humbly with our God, let us not fear the presence of doubt but welcome the opportunity it provides for us to examine our faith, strengthen our resolve, and draw nearer to the heart of God.

Shadows of Questioning: Defining and Dealing with Doubt

In the journey of faith, doubt often emerges like a shadow, subtly and sometimes unexpectedly. It can cast a silhouette over our beliefs, making the truths that once seemed so vivid appear dim and distant. To walk with God in spite of doubt, it is imperative to first understand its nature and then to engage with it constructively.

The Definition of Doubt

Doubt is a state of mind in suspension between faith and disbelief, involving uncertainty or distrust or lack of sureness about someone or something. This experience can arise from internal conflicts or external circumstances that challenge our convictions. Doubt is not the opposite of faith but rather an element within the spectrum of belief, where the assurance of what we hope for and the certainty of what we do not see (Hebrews 11:1) is at times obscured.

The Origins of Doubt

Doubt can originate from a myriad of sources: personal trials, intellectual inquiries, emotional upheavals, or spiritual warfare. The prophet Elijah, for instance, faced a profound crisis of faith after his victory on Mount Carmel. His flight into the wilderness and his subsequent despair (1 Kings 19:4) underscore that even the most steadfast among us can experience the shadow of doubt when faced with overwhelming fear or disappointment.

The Spectrum of Doubt

Doubt manifests in a spectrum ranging from mild hesitancy to severe skepticism. It can involve questioning the reliability of Scripture, the goodness of Jehovah, or the reality of one's own salvation. It may be episodic, triggered by particular events, or it may be chronic, a persistent whisper that accompanies one's faith journey.

Engaging with Doubt Through Scripture

Dealing with doubt requires an intentional return to the bedrock of Scripture. The psalmists frequently expressed their doubts and fears candidly, yet they always circled back to the truths they knew about Jehovah: His steadfast love, His power, and His ultimate goodness (Psalm 42:5). Scripture serves not only as a source of answers but also as a platform for expressing our deepest questions.

The Voice of Doubt versus The Voice of Faith

It is crucial to discern between the voice of doubt and the voice of faith. The voice of doubt often speaks in the language of fear, cynicism, and suspicion, whereas the voice of faith speaks in the language of hope, trust, and perseverance. Recognizing the source and tone of these inner dialogues can aid believers in choosing which voice to amplify and which to challenge.

The Role of Prayer in Doubt

Prayer is an essential practice in the life of a believer grappling with doubt. It is in the honest pouring out of our hearts before Jehovah that we find solace and strength. When the father of the demon-possessed boy cried out to Jesus, "I do believe; help me overcome my unbelief!" (Mark 9:24), he modeled the kind of vulnerable faith that acknowledges doubt while simultaneously seeking to overcome it through divine assistance.

The Importance of Community

The community of believers provides an essential support network for those wrestling with doubt. It offers a space for shared experiences, encouragement, and the kind of fellowship that reminds us we are not alone in our struggles. When Thomas expressed his doubts, it was in the context of the community of disciples that he found the answers he sought (John 20:24-29).

The Process of Refinement

Doubt can serve as a refining fire, purifying and strengthening our faith. It compels us to examine what we believe and why we believe it, leading to a faith that is not blind but informed, robust, and resilient. As gold is tested by fire, so too is faith tested by the challenges it endures, including the challenge of doubt (1 Peter 1:6-7).

The Power of Perseverance

Perseverance through periods of doubt is a powerful testimony to the enduring nature of faith. It is not the absence of doubt that defines the strength of our faith, but our willingness to continue walking with Jehovah even when certainty eludes us. The commitment to press on, to keep seeking, and to maintain one's confidence in Jehovah is the hallmark of a faith that endures.

The Necessity of Patience

Patience with oneself and the process is necessary when dealing with doubt. Spiritual growth, like any growth, requires time, and the resolution of doubt may not come quickly or easily. It is in the patient waiting on Jehovah that believers often find the grace and insight needed to navigate the shadows of questioning (Psalm 27:14).

Conclusion: The Light Beyond the Shadows

In conclusion, defining and dealing with doubt is an integral part of walking with God. "Walk Humbly with Your God: Putting God's

Purpose First in Your Life" seeks to guide believers through the shadows of questioning, encouraging them to face doubt with honesty, to seek understanding through Scripture, to engage in persistent prayer, to find support in community, to allow their faith to be refined, to persevere with patience, and ultimately to find reassurance in the steadfast character of Jehovah. In doing so, believers may find that the very doubts that once threatened to undermine their faith can lead to a deeper, more confident walk with God.

CHAPTER 12 Do Not Give Up in Your Walk with God!

The Resolve to Continue: Overcoming Spiritual Fatigue

In the Christian walk, spiritual fatigue can often become an unwelcome companion. It sneaks upon even the most devout believers, causing their steps to falter and their zeal to wane. It's a state of weariness where the once-clear calling of God seems to echo faintly in the chambers of a tired soul. But within the framework of persistent faith, there is a wellspring of strength that allows us to overcome this spiritual lethargy and continue with renewed vigor on the path laid out for us by Jehovah.

The Nature of Spiritual Fatigue

Spiritual fatigue is not simply a lack of physical rest or emotional comfort; it is a depletion of spiritual vitality. This can manifest as a diminished desire for prayer, a disconnection from worship, or a sense of disillusionment with one's spiritual practices. It's the wearying effect of a race that seems to stretch beyond the horizon, where the finish line is obscured by the trials and tribulations of life.

The Biblical Recognition of Fatigue

Scripture does not shy away from the reality of spiritual fatigue. Elijah, after his confrontation with the prophets of Baal, found himself exhausted and questioning under a broom tree (1 Kings 19:4). The Apostle Paul acknowledged his own trials, speaking of being "hard pressed on every side, but not crushed; perplexed, but not in despair" (2 Corinthians 4:8). These acknowledgments validate the reality of spiritual fatigue while simultaneously offering a prelude to the hope of renewal.

The Causes of Spiritual Fatigue

Several factors contribute to spiritual fatigue. It may be the result of unrelenting trials, unresolved conflict within one's faith community, or personal setbacks. Moreover, a misalignment between one's actions and God's purpose can lead to a draining sense of purposelessness. It's the chaffing of the soul's sandals from walking a path strewn with the sharp stones of doubt and disillusionment.

The Antidote to Fatigue: Divine Strength

In the face of such fatigue, the believer is not left to their own devices. Isaiah offers a powerful antidote: "But those who hope in the Lord will renew their strength. They will soar on wings like eagles; they will run and not grow weary, they will walk and not be faint" (Isaiah 40:31). This divine strength transcends human limitations and renews the weary with celestial power.

The Role of Prayer in Renewal

Prayer is the believer's lifeline to Jehovah, the channel through which spiritual fatigue is brought before the throne of grace. It is in the act of prayer that one can lay bare the tiredness of the soul and receive the "peace of God, which transcends all understanding" (Philippians 4:7). The psalmist's cries, "Out of the depths I cry to you, Lord" (Psalm 130:1), exemplify the earnest seeking of God's refreshing in the midst of spiritual exhaustion.

The Importance of God's Word

The Scriptures are not merely historical records or moral guidebooks; they are the living words that speak into the weary corners of the human heart. The Word of God is "alive and active" (Hebrews 4:12), providing guidance and encouragement, correction, and comfort. It is the bread that nourishes and the water that quenches the thirst of a soul suffering from spiritual malnourishment.

The Support of Fellowship

The resolve to continue is often strengthened by the companionship of fellow believers. The New Testament church "devoted themselves to the apostles' teaching and to fellowship, to the breaking of bread and to prayer" (Acts 2:42), recognizing the power of communal support. As the body of Christ, believers are called to bear one another's burdens (Galatians 6:2), offering strength and encouragement to those who are tired.

The Pursuit of Service

Serving others can also serve as a remedy for spiritual fatigue. In the act of giving, there is a paradoxical receiving; as Jesus said, "It is more blessed to give than to receive" (Acts 20:35). Engaging in acts of love and service redirects focus from inward struggles to the needs of others, providing a respite from self-focused weariness.

The Commitment to Perseverance

Perseverance is not simply a passive endurance but an active expression of faith. It is the choice to keep placing one foot in front of the other, trusting in Jehovah's promises and the surety of His guidance. As the Apostle Paul exhorted, "Let us not become weary in doing good, for at the proper time we will reap a harvest if we do not give up" (Galatians 6:9). This is the resolve to continue despite fatigue.

The Expectation of Restoration

The Christian faith is marked by a profound hope in restoration and renewal. It's the promise that, in the end, Jehovah will "restore, confirm, strengthen, and establish you" (1 Peter 5:10). Spiritual fatigue is but a temporary condition in the light of God's eternal promise of restoration.

Spiritual fatigue is an acknowledged and natural aspect of the human condition, even for the believer. But the journey does not end in weariness. By turning to prayer, immersing oneself in the Scriptures, engaging in fellowship, serving others, committing to perseverance, and holding fast to the hope of divine restoration, the believer can renew their strength. It is through these means that one may overcome spiritual fatigue and continue walking humbly with God, putting His purpose first in life. This is the path to a flourishing faith, where God's purpose prevails and personal growth abounds.

Persevere in Prayer: The Tenacity of Faith

The spiritual discipline of prayer stands as the bulwark of a believer's life, epitomizing the tenacity of faith that marks a profound relationship with God. Prayer is not a passive act but an active engagement with the Divine, a persistent dialogue that reflects trust and reliance on Jehovah.

The Vitality of Persistent Prayer

Persistent prayer is an expression of unwavering faith, indicative of a heart that relentlessly seeks God's presence and will. It's a robust echo of the soul's yearning, not easily quelled by adversity or delay. The vitality of such prayer is reflected in the counsel of 1 Thessalonians 5:17, which encourages believers to "pray without ceasing." This unceasing prayer is not about the constancy of spoken words but the persistence of a heart attuned to God.

Understanding the Essence of Tenacious Prayer

Tenacious prayer is characterized by its steadfast nature—a relentless pursuit of God's attention and intervention. It embodies the spirit of the widow in Jesus' parable (Luke 18:1-8), who persistently appealed to the unjust judge until she received justice. Her persistence was commended as a model for how believers should approach God in prayer, not in a manner that implies God is unjust, but to illustrate the kind of persistent faith that pleases Him.

The Challenge of Delay in Answered Prayers

One of the most challenging aspects of persistent prayer is navigating the silence or delay in receiving answers from Jehovah. It's here that many falter, misconstruing silence for neglect. Yet, Scripture teaches that delays are not denials; they are often opportunities for growth and deepening faith. In the delay, the believer's resolve is refined, and trust is deepened, as illustrated in the experience of Abraham, who waited decades for the fulfillment of God's promise of a son.

Embracing the Mystery of Divine Will

Persistent prayer also involves the humble acceptance that Jehovah's ways and timings are incomprehensible. As Isaiah 55:8-9 reminds us, "For my thoughts are not your thoughts, neither are your ways my ways," declares the Lord. "As the heavens are higher than the earth, so are my ways higher than your ways and my thoughts than your thoughts." In the face of mystery, tenacious prayer clings to the assurance that God's will is perfect, even when it deviates from human expectations.

The Intimacy of Continual Communion

Persevering in prayer is not merely about petitioning God but about cultivating an intimacy with Him. It's a dialogue that involves listening as much as speaking, a communion that acknowledges God's sovereignty while expressing the intimate desires of the heart. This continual communion fosters a deepening relationship with Jehovah, wherein the believer comes to know the heart of God as well as His voice.

The Assurance Found in Scriptural Promises

The Bible is replete with promises that bolster the believer's confidence in the efficacy of persistent prayer. Jesus assures in Matthew 7:7-8, "Ask and it will be given to you; seek and you will find; knock and the door will be opened to you." These words are not a blank check for any request, but a guarantee that when requests are aligned with God's will, they will be granted in His perfect timing.

The Role of the Holy Spirit in Prayer

While the Bible does not teach that the Holy Spirit indwells believers, it does present the Holy Spirit as a helper in prayer. Romans 8:26 speaks of the Spirit interceding for believers in accordance with God's will. This intercession reflects the assistance believers receive in prayer, ensuring that their petitions are in harmony with Jehovah's purposes.

The Testimony of Prayer in Perseverance

Throughout history, the testimony of many believers serves as a beacon of encouragement in the pursuit of tenacious prayer. The accounts of Daniel praying earnestly in the face of potential death, or David's numerous psalms of lament and subsequent praise, are enduring examples of the power of persistent prayer.

The Transformation through Persistent Prayer

Finally, persistent prayer is transformative. It not only changes circumstances but also changes the one who prays. Through continual engagement with Jehovah, the believer is shaped into the image of Christ, learning to rely not on their understanding but on God's provision and guidance.

In the discipline of persistent prayer, believers find the tenacity of faith to navigate the complexities of their walk with God. They are called to engage continually with Jehovah, not as a duty but as a privilege. It is in the constancy of this divine conversation that believers are equipped to put God's purpose first in their lives, embracing His will and timing with unwavering trust. As they do so, they discover the profound depths of a relationship with God and the boundless potential for personal growth and spiritual maturation. Such is the journey for those who choose to walk humbly with their God, undeterred by the trials of life and strengthened by the power of prayer.

CHAPTER 13 Those Who Lack Faith Cannot Walk with God

The Necessity of Belief: Foundations for the Journey

Faith is the bedrock of a believer's walk with God; it is the prerequisite for any genuine relationship with the Divine. Without faith, one cannot begin to fathom the depths of a spiritual journey, nor can they align with the purposes and will of Jehovah. The necessity of belief in God as the foundational element of one's spiritual journey is a theme consistently woven throughout Scripture.

Faith as the Starting Point

The Scripture unequivocally states in Hebrews 11:6 that "without faith it is impossible to please Him, for he who comes to God must believe that He is, and that He is a rewarder of those who diligently seek Him." This verse serves as a clarion call to all who would embark on the journey of walking humbly with their God. It isn't a mere acknowledgment of God's existence but a deep-seated conviction that Jehovah is the sovereign Lord of all, worthy of our trust and obedience.

The Role of Faith in Understanding Divine Purpose

Understanding and accepting God's purpose for one's life begins with belief. Belief is not simply an intellectual assent but a surrender of one's whole being to the truth of Jehovah's sovereignty and righteousness. It is through this lens of faith that we can begin to discern and embrace God's purposes, as seen in the lives of biblical figures like Moses, who "endured as seeing Him who is invisible" (Hebrews 11:27).

The Character of Biblical Faith

The character of biblical faith is often misunderstood. It is not blind trust nor wishful thinking. Instead, biblical faith is a confident assurance in the character and promises of God, despite the current circumstances or unseen outcomes. It is this assurance that undergirded the faith of Abraham when he was called to leave his homeland for a place he would later receive as an inheritance, "and he went out, not knowing where he was going" (Hebrews 11:8).

Belief Manifested Through Action

Belief is not passive; it demands action. Just as faith without works is dead, a proclaimed belief that does not translate into a walk consistent with God's commandments is futile (James 2:26). One's faith is authenticated by their deeds, and thus, belief serves as the foundation upon which the structure of godly living is built.

The Conviction of Things Not Seen

The journey with God is one that often transcends the visible and tangible. Faith involves the "conviction of things not seen," a profound trust in Jehovah's governance of the universe and the unfolding of His divine plan, even when our eyes cannot behold the evidence of such orchestration.

The Test of Faith Through Trials

The resolve to maintain belief in the face of trials is another cornerstone of the journey. As believers, the assurance of our faith is tested through adversities, just as gold is tested by fire. This concept is beautifully illustrated in the life of Job, whose faith was tested to extreme measures yet remained steadfast, reflecting an unyielding trust in the character and wisdom of God.

The Assurance of God's Faithfulness

Belief is sustained by the assurance of Jehovah's faithfulness. The Bible chronicles the faithfulness of God throughout history, offering believers a record of His unwavering constancy. This record serves as both a reminder and a promise that He who has been faithful will continue to be so, anchoring the believer's faith amidst the vicissitudes of life.

The Personalization of Faith

While faith is a communal concept, embodied within the body of believers, it is also profoundly personal. It requires a personalized trust in Jehovah, a relationship that is as unique as the individual. The Psalms often reflect this personal aspect of faith, with expressions of deep trust and personal reliance on God's lovingkindness and mercy.

The Growth of Belief Over Time

Belief is not static; it is dynamic and expected to grow. The journey with God is one of continuous development, where faith is stretched and expanded. This is evident in the life of Peter, whose faith matured over time from impetuous actions to a solid rock upon which the early church could lean.

The Fruitfulness of a Believer's Life

A life built on the foundation of belief in Jehovah will be fruitful. This fruitfulness is not merely measured by worldly success but by the spiritual fruit that grows from a life lived in harmony with God's will—love, joy, peace, patience, kindness, goodness, faithfulness, gentleness, and self-control (Galatians 5:22-23).

In sum, belief is the indispensable foundation for anyone desiring to walk with God. It is the starting point, the sustainer, and the source of growth in the believer's life. Without it, one cannot hope to grasp the purpose of Jehovah, endure the trials that test our faith, or produce the spiritual fruit that characterizes a life in communion with God. As we seek to put God's purpose first, belief is not merely an introductory step; it is the ongoing sustenance for every step of the journey that lies ahead.

Faithless Wanderings: The Implications of Doubt

In the narrative of walking with God, the presence of faith is as crucial as the need for a compass during a voyage at sea. Without it, the journey becomes aimless, and the traveler is prone to wander. To walk with God is to navigate life's complexities and uncertainties with the assurance of His guidance and promises. When faith falters, doubt creeps in, and with it comes a myriad of implications that can disrupt our spiritual trajectory.

The Intrinsic Connection Between Faith and Direction

Doubt, in its essence, signifies a loss of direction. It is the cloud that obscures the stars by which sailors navigate. In the spiritual journey, these stars are the promises of Jehovah, and faith is the assurance that, though unseen, they are steadfast and reliable. Doubt muddies this assurance, leading to wandering—a movement without purpose or clear destination.

The Paralysis of Spiritual Progress

A lack of faith does not merely redirect one's path; it often halts progress entirely. The Israelites, due to doubt, spent 40 years wandering in the wilderness, a journey that should have taken mere weeks (Numbers 14:33-34). Their doubt in Jehovah's provision and protection paralyzed them with fear and resulted in a generation that never saw the Promised Land. The same is true for modern believers; doubt can cause stagnation in spiritual growth and fruitfulness.

The Breeding Ground for Disobedience

When doubt enters the heart, it becomes fertile ground for disobedience. This is not a mere correlation but a causal relationship. Doubt undermines trust in Jehovah and His commandments, making room for the individual's own understanding to take precedence. This can be seen in the account of Saul, who, doubting the prophet Samuel's return, offered the burnt offering himself, a direct violation of God's command, leading to his downfall (1 Samuel 13:8-14).

The Impact on Witness and Testimony

The implications of doubt stretch beyond the individual to the collective witness of God's people. A faithless wanderer's life becomes a blurred reflection of Jehovah's character, dimming the light meant to guide others to the truth. The testimony of a believer filled with doubt does little to persuade others of the reality and goodness of God.

The Erosion of Relationship with God

At the heart of the matter is the relational impact of doubt. Walking with God presupposes communion, a close-knit fellowship built on trust. Doubt erodes this trust, distancing the believer from Jehovah, not unlike Adam and Eve who, after their transgression borne of doubt, hid from God's presence (Genesis 3:8).

The Emotional and Mental Toll of Doubt

The wanderings of a faithless heart are not without emotional and mental consequence. Anxiety, fear, and confusion often accompany doubt, as seen in Elijah's despair under the broom tree (1 Kings 19:4). Without the anchor of faith, the soul is left to drift on the tumultuous seas of human frailty and uncertainty.

The Diminished Capacity for Godly Discernment

Faith provides spiritual discernment, a divine lens through which we can perceive and interpret life's events. Doubt distorts this lens, making it difficult to distinguish between God's guidance and mere human opinion or deception. The lack of spiritual discernment is vividly portrayed in the life of Samson, who, blinded by his desires, could not see the source of his strength was his covenant with Jehovah (Judges 16:20).

The Undermining of Effective Prayer

James reminds us that the one who doubts is like a wave of the sea, driven and tossed by the wind, and should not expect to receive anything from the Lord (James 1:6-7). Prayer, one of the vital lifelines in a believer's walk with God, becomes ineffective when marred by doubt, as the necessary ingredient of faith is missing.

The Challenge of Community and Fellowship

Doubt does not only isolate us from Jehovah but also fractures the fellowship with fellow believers. The unity of faith that binds the community of God's people together is weakened when members begin to waver in their convictions. This is exemplified in the dissension and disunity that emerged in the early church when members doubted the apostolic teachings (Acts 20:29-30).

The Disintegration of Hope

Finally, the most grievous implication of doubt is the disintegration of hope. Faith is the substance of things hoped for, the evidence of things not seen (Hebrews 11:1). When doubt erases the assurance that faith provides, hope fades. Without hope, the believer's walk becomes a trudge, a tiresome plodding without anticipation of the joy set before us—the ultimate fulfillment of Jehovah's promises.

In conclusion, to wander faithlessly is to drift aimlessly, cut off from the life-giving waters of trust in Jehovah. It has serious and far-reaching implications, affecting not only the individual believer's relationship with God but also their influence on others, their emotional well-being, and their eternal destiny. The antidote to such wandering is a steadfast faith, which clings unwaveringly to the promises of God, even in the face of life's fiercest storms. As we proceed in writing "Walk Humbly with Your God: Putting God's Purpose First in Your Life," we delve further into the practicalities of nurturing and maintaining such faith, that our walk may be steady and our path straight, guided by the infallible Word of God.

CHAPTER 14 Let Us Never Shrink Back from Our Walk with God

Fortified Steps: Standing Firm in Your Spiritual Journey

The Christian walk is a voyage that requires both the grace of God and the resolute steps of the believer. To stand firm in one's spiritual journey is to understand and engage in a battle that is not against flesh and blood, but against spiritual forces that seek to undermine our faith (Ephesians 6:12). The fortification of our steps does not come from our strength but is built on the solid rock of our faith in Jehovah and His Word.

The Bedrock of the Scriptures

The Scriptures provide the believer with a firm foundation. When the winds of doubt and the storms of life assail us, it is the truth of God's Word that anchors our souls. We are reminded of the wise man who built his house upon the rock; when the rain descended, and the floods came, and the winds blew and beat upon that house, it did not fall, for it was founded upon a rock (Matthew 7:24-25). This rock represents the unchanging and infallible Word of Jehovah. Our spiritual fortification begins with a steadfast commitment to study, meditate upon, and apply the Scriptures in our daily lives.

The Shield of Faith

Faith acts as a shield, protecting us from the fiery darts of the wicked one (Ephesians 6:16). It is a confident assurance in the character and promises of Jehovah, a trust that goes beyond intellectual assent to a deep-seated conviction that stands against the tides of skepticism and fear. The journey of Abraham stands as a testament to this; he "did not waver through unbelief regarding the promise of God, but was strengthened in his faith and gave glory to God" (Romans 4:20). His trust in Jehovah's promise fortified his steps, even when the fulfillment of that promise seemed humanly impossible.

The Practice of Perseverance

Perseverance is the practice of persistent endurance in the face of challenges. The Bible encourages us to run with perseverance the race marked out for us, fixing our eyes on Jesus, the pioneer and perfecter of faith (Hebrews 12:1-2). Our spiritual journey is not a sprint but a marathon, and standing firm requires a steady, enduring faith that refuses to give in to weariness or despair.

The Strength of a Godly Character

The development of a godly character is crucial for standing firm. The Apostle Peter speaks of adding to our faith goodness, knowledge, self-control, perseverance, godliness, mutual affection, and love (2 Peter 1:5-7). Each of these qualities acts as a reinforcing bar in the concrete of our spiritual lives, making us resilient in the face of temptation and adversity. A character molded by divine attributes is less likely to crumble when confronted with the pressures of life.

The Support of Godly Fellowship

We are not meant to walk alone. The early church thrived on fellowship, breaking bread from house to house, and sharing with those in need (Acts 2:46-47). A community of believers provides mutual encouragement, accountability, and support. As iron sharpens iron, so one person sharpens another (Proverbs 27:17). In times of weakness, it is often the strength of our brothers and sisters in Christ that helps us stand firm.

The Armor of God

The Apostle Paul describes the armor of God as essential for taking a stand against the devil's schemes (Ephesians 6:11-17). This includes truth, righteousness, the gospel of peace, faith, salvation, and the Word of God. Each piece of this armor is not merely symbolic but represents tangible aspects of a life wholly surrendered to Jehovah. It is through the daily donning of this armor that we are prepared to stand firm, no matter what spiritual battles we may face.

The Power of Prayer

Prayer is our direct line of communication with Jehovah. It is the means by which we draw strength from Him and align our will with His. The life of Jesus exemplified this; despite His divinity, He frequently withdrew to lonely places and prayed (Luke 5:16). In our own journey, prayer is not an occasional exercise but a continuous, life-sustaining practice that fortifies our steps.

The Assurance of Jehovah's Sovereignty

Understanding that Jehovah is sovereign over all aspects of life instills confidence in the believer. Nothing happens outside of His will or His control. The psalmist proclaimed, "Though I walk in the midst of trouble, you preserve my life" (Psalm 138:7). The assurance of God's sovereignty is a firm support to those who are walking with Him, allowing them to stand unshaken amid life's uncertainties.

The Witness of Steadfast Believers

The annals of Christian history are filled with the accounts of men and women who stood firm in their faith against insurmountable odds. The Apostles, the early church martyrs, and countless others throughout the ages have displayed extraordinary courage and faithfulness. These witnesses serve as a cloud of testimonies, encouraging us to "run with perseverance the race marked out for us" (Hebrews 12:1).

In the course of "Walk Humbly with Your God: Putting God's Purpose First in Your Life," we must emphasize that to never shrink back from our walk with Jehovah requires a fortification of our spiritual lives. Each step taken in faith, grounded in Scripture, clothed with godly character, and supported by the body of Christ, is a step that resounds through the heavens. It is a declaration that we are Jehovah's, and in His strength, we will stand firm to the end.

Unretractable Faith: The Commitment to Forward Motion

In the realm of spirituality and the pursuit of walking with God, one encounters the concept of unretractable faith. This is not a stagnant belief, but a dynamic, living commitment that propels the believer ever forward in their journey with Jehovah. It is a faith that does not retreat but moves with a steadfastness that is evident throughout the narratives of Scripture and the lived experiences of countless followers of Jehovah over millennia.

The Essence of Unretractable Faith

Unretractable faith is characterized by a relentless commitment to progress in one's spiritual life, regardless of the challenges that may arise. It is a faith that echoes the determination of Paul the Apostle, who declared, "I press on toward the goal to win the prize for which God has called me heavenward in Christ Jesus" (Philippians 3:14). Such a faith is not merely a passive agreement with theological doctrines but is an active, living force that spurs the believer to continuous growth and steadfastness.

Forward Motion in the Face of Adversity

The Bible is replete with examples of individuals whose faith was marked by a consistent forward motion. Consider the life of Joseph, who, despite being sold into slavery by his brothers and unjustly imprisoned in Egypt, never lost his faith in Jehovah's purposes. His unwavering trust and forward-looking perspective ultimately positioned him to save not only Egypt but his own family from famine. Joseph's story is a profound example of how unretractable faith in Jehovah's sovereign plan keeps one moving forward, even when circumstances seem to pull backward.

The Proactive Nature of Faith

A faith that is unretractable does not passively wait for change but engages actively with Jehovah's will. Nehemiah, when he heard of the desolation of Jerusalem's walls, did not merely lament; he sought God in prayer and then took action, leading the effort to rebuild the walls despite opposition and threats. His faith was put into action, demonstrating that part of moving forward is a readiness to undertake the work Jehovah sets before us.

Endurance as the Hallmark of Unretractable Faith

To possess unretractable faith is to endure. Endurance is an attribute often highlighted in the New Testament, especially in the book of Hebrews, where the author exhorts believers to "run with endurance the race that is set before us" (Hebrews 12:1). This race is not a short sprint but a lifelong marathon, requiring not bursts of speed but persistent, sustained motion. The unretractable nature of faith is one that endures through trials, temptations, and tribulations, much like Jesus, who for the joy set before Him endured the cross, scorning its shame (Hebrews 12:2).

The Unchanging Object of Faith

The commitment to forward motion in faith is anchored in the unchanging nature of Jehovah, who is described as the same "yesterday, today, and forever" (Hebrews 13:8). It is this immutable character of God that assures the believer that their faith is not in vain and that the promises upon which they stand will not shift or falter. Unretractable faith draws its strength from the constancy of Jehovah, not from the changing tides of human circumstances.

Continual Learning and Growth

Unretractable faith is marked by a lifelong commitment to learning and spiritual growth. It recognizes that to stand still is to stagnate. The believer is, therefore, committed to the continual study of the Scriptures, learning from the parables of Jesus, the wisdom of the Proverbs, the prophecies of the Old Testament, and the teachings of the epistles. Each of these serves to deepen understanding and propel the believer forward in their walk with Jehovah.

The Role of Repentance and Reformation

A faith that cannot be retracted also understands the role of repentance and reformation in the life of a believer. When Peter, one of Jesus' closest disciples, denied knowing Him, he later wept bitterly in repentance. His faith, though momentarily shaken, was not retracted; instead, it moved forward, leading him to become a pillar in the early church. This shows us that unretractable faith is not about never failing but about rising each time we fall, realigning ourselves with God's will, and moving forward with renewed commitment.

The Testimony of Unretractable Faith

The life of a believer who does not shrink back is a powerful testimony to the world. It reflects the light of Jehovah's truth in a way that words alone cannot. The lives of early Christians, who despite intense persecution continued to meet together, worship, and spread the gospel, stand as a testament to a faith that is unretractable. Their commitment to forward motion despite the cost is a clarion call to believers today to hold fast to their confession of hope without wavering (Hebrews 10:23).

Unretractable Faith in the Modern World

In our modern era, with its myriad distractions and challenges to faith, the commitment to forward motion is as crucial as ever. The believer is called to navigate the complexities of life with a faith that is rooted in the unshakeable truth of Scripture and the steadfast character of Jehovah. As society shifts and morals become fluid, unretractable faith holds to the absolutes of God's word, advancing in a world that often seems to be retreating from the truth.

In conclusion, unretractable faith—the commitment to forward motion—is essential in our walk with Jehovah. It is a faith that does not look back but continually presses on towards the ultimate goal: a deep, personal, and everlasting communion with Jehovah. It is this faith that enables the believer to walk humbly with their God, to rise above the transient, and to live a life of purpose and hope. It is the cornerstone of a life lived in submission to Jehovah's will, a life that, despite its ups and downs, never shrinks back but always moves forward toward the heavenly prize.

CHAPTER 15 Christian Way of Life

The Path Lived: The Everyday of Christian Living

The Christian way of life is not defined by the occasional grand gesture or the infrequent acts of piety; it is the culmination of daily decisions, habitual actions, and the steadfast walk in the ordinary pathways of life. It's a commitment that finds expression in the regular, the mundane, and the oft-overlooked moments that collectively form the fabric of a believer's existence.

The Quiet Consistency of Devotion

In the everyday of Christian living, the quiet consistency of personal devotion holds a place of utmost importance. It is in the gentle whispers of morning prayers, the meditative reading of Scripture in the stillness of dawn, and the reflective pause to offer thanks before a meal where one's devotion is often most apparent. This consistent engagement with Jehovah is reminiscent of the Psalmist's love for the law, meditating on it "day and night" (Psalm 1:2).

Integrity in the Commonplace

The everyday of Christian life calls for integrity, not just in the grandiose moments of life but in the commonplace. It is the honesty with which a believer conducts business, the truthfulness in conversation, and the faithfulness in responsibilities, no matter how small. The life of Daniel exemplifies this, as even his detractors could find no fault with him "unless it has something to do with the law of his God" (Daniel 6:5). Thus, Christian integrity is woven into the very essence of day-to-day living.

The Fabric of Relationships

Christian living is deeply relational, and the everyday of this life is often best seen in how one interacts with others. It is found in the kindness shown to a stranger, the patience extended to a difficult family member, and the love that covers a multitude of sins within the community of faith. As the Apostle Paul exhorted the Ephesians to "be kind to one another, tenderhearted, forgiving one another, as God in Christ forgave you" (Ephesians 4:32), so the everyday Christian life is marked by a grace-filled approach to relationships.

Stewardship of Time and Resources

The management of time and resources is a tangible expression of everyday Christian living. It is a stewardship that is mindful of the temporal and eternal, investing in what bears lasting fruit. The parable of the talents (Matthew 25:14-30) serves as a powerful metaphor for this daily responsibility, encouraging believers to use what they have been given in service to Jehovah and to others, not merely for self-gain.

Witness in the Mundane

A Christian's daily conduct serves as a silent witness to the transforming power of God. It is not just the evangelistic efforts that speak of Jehovah's kingdom but the subtle reflections of His character in everyday interactions. As the early Christians' lives were dramatically changed, so their daily behavior spoke volumes, leading many to praise God (1 Peter 2:12). The mundane thus becomes a canvas for displaying the transformative work of faith.

Laboring in Love

The everyday Christian life embraces labor as an act of worship and a means of participating in God's purposes. It echoes the Thessalonian believers whom Paul commended for their "work of faith and labor of love" (1 Thessalonians 1:3). Whether in the workplace, at home, or in ministry, the labor undertaken is not for mere earthly gain but as an offering to Jehovah, recognizing that "in the Lord your labor is not in vain" (1 Corinthians 15:58).

Rest as an Act of Trust

Amidst the busyness of life, rest holds a sacred place in the rhythm of everyday Christian living. It mirrors Jehovah's own rest after the creation work and serves as a reminder that one is not sustained by toil alone. The practice of the Sabbath, though fulfilled in Christ and not legally binding to Christians, provides a principle of rest that trusts in God's provision and sovereignty over one's life.

Navigating Trials with Resilience

The inevitability of trials in the Christian life requires a daily resilience that draws on the deep wells of faith. This resilience looks not to one's own strength but to the example of Jesus, who "endured the cross, despising the shame" (Hebrews 12:2). It is a resilience that learns contentment in all circumstances, as Paul describes, knowing how to be brought low and how to abound (Philippians 4:12).

A Life of Continuous Worship

Ultimately, the everyday of Christian living is an ongoing act of worship. It is an acknowledgment that every moment, every breath, is an opportunity to glorify Jehovah. This life reflects the sentiment of the Apostle Paul who said, "So whether you eat or drink, or whatever you do, do all to the glory of God" (1 Corinthians 10:31). The path lived is thus a testament to a life that seeks to make the ordinary extraordinary through a ceaseless offering of oneself to God.

In essence, the everyday Christian life is an intricate tapestry of acts of worship, relationships, stewardship, labor, rest, and resilience. It is the precious, consistent, and often quiet display of one's faith in the small, seemingly insignificant details of daily life. As believers walk this path lived, they not only embody the teachings of Scripture but also pave the way for others to encounter the living God through the testimony of a life wholly devoted to Jehovah. It is this everyday faithfulness that undergirds a vibrant and enduring walk with God, as it is the ordinary moments that often have the most extraordinary impact on the journey of faith.

Beyond Sundays: Integrating Faith into the Fabric of Life

The Christian walk is not a once-a-week pilgrimage but a continuous journey that weaves itself into the very fabric of our daily existence. It's a vibrant faith that transcends the walls of a church and permeates every aspect of life. It is in the day-to-day life that the reality of one's faith is truly lived out and tested.

The Integration of Faith and Work

Our vocations and careers are primary fields where faith must be visible. The workplace becomes an avenue for demonstrating the principles of Scripture, where integrity, diligence, and fairness reflect the character of Jehovah. Consider the diligence of the Proverbs 31 woman, who is praised for her industriousness and wisdom in her dealings. Similarly, Christian employees and employers alike are called to work "as for the Lord and not for men" (Colossians 3:23), turning their professions into platforms for glorifying God.

Home as the Heartland of Faith

The domestic life of a believer is a profound sphere for the application of faith. Family interactions offer countless opportunities to exhibit love, patience, and sacrificial service. As the domestic church, the Christian household is where the spiritual disciplines of prayer, Bible study, and worship should be regularly practiced, establishing a firm foundation for both young and old. It echoes the directive given to the Israelites in Deuteronomy 6:7, to teach God's commands to their children "when you sit at home and when you walk along the road, when you lie down and when you get up."

Influence on Culture and Society

Christians are called to be the salt and light in the world (Matthew 5:13-16), which means engaging with society in ways that reflect the principles of Jehovah's kingdom. This could mean participating in community service, contributing to ethical practices in social spheres, or simply being a voice of wisdom and moderation in a culture often marked by extremes.

Financial Stewardship with Eternal Perspective

How believers manage their finances also speaks volumes about their faith. Financial decisions should be guided by the principles of generosity, stewardship, and trust in Jehovah's provision. The Macedonian church, despite their extreme poverty, exemplified this as they gave generously to support fellow believers (2 Corinthians 8:1-5). A Christian's budget and spending habits, therefore, become a testament to their values and priorities.

Recreational Activities and Rest

Faith finds its way even into leisure and rest, shaping how Christians choose to spend their downtime. It involves selecting activities that are wholesome, that build up rather than tear down, and that offer restorative rest in the Lord rather than mere escapism. Jesus Himself took time away to rest and pray, setting a precedent for balancing ministry and personal well-being (Mark 6:31-32).

The Role of Technology and Media

In a world saturated with technology and media, Christians are challenged to integrate their faith by selecting content that edifies and by using these powerful tools to spread the good news of the gospel. This discernment in media consumption reflects the call to "set no worthless thing before your eyes" (Psalm 101:3) and to use speech—or in this case, digital communication—that is edifying (Ephesians 4:29).

Dealing with Secular Ideologies

Christians are constantly interacting with a plethora of worldviews and ideologies. Integrating faith into daily life means evaluating these ideas critically through the lens of Scripture and holding firmly to biblical truths. Like the Bereans who examined the Scriptures daily to see if what Paul said was true (Acts 17:11), believers today are to engage with secular thought with both open minds and discerning hearts.

Navigating Relationships with Unbelievers

The Christian is often in the position of maintaining relationships with those who do not share their faith. These interactions, conducted with grace and truth, can be powerful witnesses to the gospel. The approach of Jesus with the Samaritan woman at the well (John 4:1-26) serves as an exemplary model of engaging in meaningful conversation while maintaining one's commitment to truth.

Continuous Spiritual Growth

The believer's life is one of ongoing spiritual development. Integrating faith into daily life includes regular self-examination, prayer, and continual learning from Scripture. It's a dynamic process, where one is "transformed by the renewing of your mind" (Romans 12:2) and growing "in the grace and knowledge of our Lord and Savior Jesus Christ" (2 Peter 3:18).

Facing Trials with a Godly Perspective

When trials arise, as they inevitably will, the fabric of our daily lives reveals the strength of our faith. A Christian's response to adversity should echo that of Job, who, despite immense suffering, could still say, "Though he slay me, yet will I trust in him" (Job 13:15). It is this unwavering trust in Jehovah's sovereignty and goodness that characterizes a faith that extends beyond Sundays.

In summary, integrating faith into the fabric of life is about allowing every thought, word, and action to be a reflection of one's relationship with God. It's about seeking Jehovah's will in every decision and acknowledging Him in all our ways (Proverbs 3:6). It's about living out the teachings of Scripture so consistently and authentically that one's life cannot help but proclaim the gospel. As such, the Christian way of life is not a separate aspect of existence but the very essence of all that we do, every day, in every way.

CHAPTER 16 Walk in Wisdom Toward Outsiders

Navigating Relationships: Wisdom in Witness

In the Christian life, one of the most critical aspects of demonstrating our faith is in how we relate to and engage with those who do not share our beliefs. As believers, we are ambassadors for Christ (2 Corinthians 5:20), and thus, our interactions with outsiders are not just incidental; they are opportunities for witness and testament to our relationship with Jehovah.

The Foundation of Wisdom in Relationships

The Scripture counsels us to "walk in wisdom toward outsiders" (Colossians 4:5). This wisdom is not of this world but is from above, characterized by purity, peace, gentleness, openness to reason, mercy, and good fruits (James 3:17). When engaging with those outside the faith, the Christian must lean heavily on this wisdom, which is first and foremost grounded in the fear of Jehovah—a fear that is not a terrified trepidation but a profound respect and reverence for God's holiness and authority.

Communication with Grace and Salt

Our speech should always be gracious, seasoned with salt (Colossians 4:6). This implies that our words must be both edifying and preservative. As salt preserves food from corruption, so should our words help preserve the moral and spiritual integrity of our conversations. Speaking with grace means our interactions are characterized by kindness and compassion, never compromising truth but always expressing it in love.

Demonstrating Godly Character

In every encounter with non-believers, Christians are called to exhibit the fruit of the Spirit: love, joy, peace, patience, kindness, goodness, faithfulness, gentleness, and self-control (Galatians 5:22-23). It is not merely about winning an argument or imposing a viewpoint; it is about displaying the transformation that God has wrought in our lives. This transformation is often the most powerful witness.

Engaging with Cultural Sensitivity

In navigating relationships with those from different cultural or religious backgrounds, wisdom calls for sensitivity and understanding. Like Paul in Athens, who acknowledged the religiosity of the people and even quoted their own poets (Acts 17:22-28), we should find common ground where possible and build bridges for the gospel.

Empathy in Witnessing

Empathy is key in relating to others, especially in witnessing. Just as Jesus wept with Mary and Martha before raising Lazarus (John 11:35), we are to weep with those who weep and rejoice with those who rejoice (Romans 12:15). This empathy opens hearts and can lead to opportunities for deeper conversations about faith.

Living the Gospel Before Speaking It

Actions often speak louder than words, and this is profoundly true in Christian witness. By living a life that is in line with the teachings of the Bible, believers offer a silent yet potent testimony to their faith. Our deeds should match our words, as James points out that faith without works is dead (James 2:26). When outsiders see the love and good works emanating from a believer's life, it glorifies Jehovah and draws them to inquire about the hope that we have (1 Peter 3:15).

Navigating Difficult Conversations

There will be times when believers are confronted with challenging questions or even hostility. In these moments, wisdom in witness requires a response that is gentle and respectful, keeping a clear conscience so that those who speak maliciously against your good behavior in Christ may be ashamed of their slander (1 Peter 3:16). It is not about defeating an opponent but about representing Christ well.

Wisdom in Digital Spaces

In our increasingly digital world, how we conduct ourselves online is also a crucial aspect of our witness. Social media platforms and other digital spaces can be arenas for much conflict and strife. However, a Christian's online presence should be marked by the same grace and wisdom that characterizes their physical interactions.

Consistency in Public and Private

Consistency between our public witness and our private lives is crucial. There can be no dichotomy between who we are before others and who we are in the secret places of our lives. As it is written, we are to be the same in public as we are in private, for Jehovah sees all (Hebrews 4:13). This integrity is fundamental to a credible witness.

Prayerful Dependence on God

In all efforts to navigate relationships wisely, believers must rely on prayer, recognizing that it is God who works in the hearts of people. As we engage with others, our dependence on God through prayer acknowledges that we do not witness in our own strength but in the strength that God supplies (1 Peter 4:11).

In summary, navigating relationships with wisdom as witnesses for Christ is about embodying the gospel in every aspect of our lives. It involves speaking and acting in ways that reflect the heart of Jehovah, using our lives as living epistles (2 Corinthians 3:2-3) known and read by all. In doing so, we provide a compelling testimony to the transforming power of the gospel, sowing seeds that, in God's timing, may bear fruit unto eternal life.

Bridges, Not Barriers: Engaging Others with Grace and Insight

In the tapestry of human interactions, Christians are called not to be artisans who build walls but rather bridge-builders who connect, extend grace, and share insight across the chasms of belief, tradition, and culture. This approach to engaging others is not only about being polite but about being Christ-like in our demeanor and actions, reflecting a life transformed by the power of the gospel.

The Essence of Grace in Engagement

Grace is the unmerited favor we have received from Jehovah, and it is this same grace that should flow through us to others. In extending grace to those outside of the faith, we must remember that "while we were still sinners, Christ died for us" (Romans 5:8). If Jehovah showed such love to us before we turned to Him, we ought to demonstrate patience and kindness to those who have yet to accept the truth.

Insight Born of Understanding

To engage with insight, one must seek to understand the perspectives and backgrounds of others. Consider the approach of the Apostle Paul when he addressed the diverse audience on Mars Hill (Acts 17). He had taken the time to understand their beliefs and used that knowledge to connect their search for truth to the gospel. He did not start by condemning their idols but by pointing to an altar dedicated "to an unknown god" and used that as a bridge to introduce them to Jehovah, the true God.

The Role of Empathy in Building Bridges

Jesus exemplified empathy in His ministry. He met people where they were, both physically and spiritually. When speaking with the

Samaritan woman at the well (John 4), He crossed social and cultural barriers to engage her in a life-changing conversation. His insight into her life and His offer of "living water" demonstrated a profound understanding of her deepest needs.

Dialogue, Not Monologue

Engaging others with grace and insight is not about talking at them but with them. It is about creating a dialogue where both parties feel heard and respected. Jesus' conversation with Nicodemus (John 3) shows a respectful and inquisitive dialogue. Jesus answered his questions and led him gently to deeper truths, unveiling the necessity of being "born again" to see the kingdom of God.

Living as Exemplars of Christ's Love

The early Christians were known for their love for one another—a love that was attractive to outsiders and drew them to the faith (John 13:35). When we live out this love genuinely, we become living testimonies of God's grace and truth. People are often more persuaded by what they see in our lives than by what they hear from our lips.

Conflict Resolution with a Healing Touch

Disagreements and conflicts will arise, but Christians are called to handle disputes differently. The way we resolve conflicts can build bridges rather than create barriers. The wisdom from above, which is "first pure, then peaceable" (James 3:17), guides us to pursue reconciliation with a spirit of gentleness and respect, seeking to heal rather than to win.

Sharing Insights from Scripture

When sharing insights from Scripture, it is important to do so in a way that invites others to explore the Bible for themselves. Rather than merely providing answers, we should encourage others to ask questions and seek understanding. When Philip encountered the Ethiopian eunuch reading Isaiah, he asked, "Do you understand what you are reading?" (Acts 8:30). This opened the door for a discussion that led to the eunuch's conversion.

Guarding Against Cultural Insensitivity

As we engage with individuals from various cultures and walks of life, we must be careful not to impose our cultural understanding upon the gospel message. Our aim is to present the unchanging truth of Scripture in a way that is relevant and comprehensible to different cultural contexts, just as the gospel was spread throughout the diverse cultures of the New Testament world.

Fostering a Spirit of Inclusivity

In the body of Christ, there is no room for partiality or exclusion (James 2:1-9). As such, our engagement with outsiders should reflect a spirit of inclusivity that mirrors Jehovah's impartiality. Each person, made in the image of God, should be treated with dignity and respect, with the understanding that the gospel is for "every nation and tribe and language and people" (Revelation 14:6).

Cultivating Cultural Intelligence

Cultural intelligence is the ability to relate and work effectively across cultures. In Christian ministry, this means understanding and respecting the customs and traditions of those we are reaching out to, while still holding fast to biblical truth. It's not about compromising our message, but about contextualizing it in a way that is understandable and relevant to the listener's situation.

The Power of Personal Testimony

Sharing personal stories of faith and transformation can be powerful in building bridges. When we share how Jehovah has worked in our lives, we offer something that is not merely theoretical but experiential and authentic. These testimonies resonate with people because they reveal the personal and relational nature of God.

Avoiding Arguments and Embracing Gentle Persuasion

It is written, "A servant of the Lord must not quarrel but be gentle to all" (2 Timothy 2:24). Our conversations should not be about winning arguments but about gently guiding others towards truth. As we engage in dialogue, our words should be seasoned with salt—that is, spoken with wisdom and grace—so that we may know how to answer each person (Colossians 4:6).

In summary, building bridges requires a blend of grace, empathy, dialogue, and a Christ-like example. As Christians, we must navigate the waters of engagement with the wisdom that comes from above, always ready to extend the hand of fellowship across the divide, that we may draw others to the truth and love that is found in Jehovah and His Word.

CHAPTER 17 'Paying Close Attention as to How We Walk

Mindful Steps: The Intentionality of Spiritual Conduct

In the journey of faith, the manner in which one walks does not refer to the physical act of placing one foot in front of the other, but rather the spiritual discipline of aligning every aspect of life with the will and Word of Jehovah. It's a daily commitment to live not by chance but with deliberate purpose according to divine guidance.

The Deliberate Walk

Walking in a manner worthy of the calling received (Ephesians 4:1) necessitates intentionality. It's about choosing paths of righteousness, making decisions with the awareness of Jehovah's presence, and conducting oneself in ways that honor Him. This purposeful walk is akin to the careful steps one would take when navigating a narrow ridge, fully aware that each step has significant consequences.

Conduct Rooted in Scripture

Spiritual conduct must be deeply rooted in Scripture, which "is breathed out by God and profitable for teaching, for reproof, for correction, and for training in righteousness" (2 Timothy 3:16). To walk mindfully in the Lord's ways, one must first know what those ways are, which requires diligent study and application of the Bible. It is not enough to simply read the Word; it must be lived out in practical, everyday actions.

The Thoughtful Reflection of Actions

To live intentionally is to reflect thoughtfully on one's actions and their impact on others. It is to be like Daniel, who "purposed in his heart that he would not defile himself" (Daniel 1:8), and therefore made choices that reflected his commitment to Jehovah, even when such choices were countercultural and difficult.

The Regular Examination of Motives

Spiritual conduct is also about regularly examining one's motives, ensuring they align with God's purposes. This introspection is not meant to be self-absorbed but self-aware, recognizing that the heart is "deceitful above all things" (Jeremiah 17:9), and requires the light of Jehovah's truth to discern its true condition.

The Conscious Repudiation of Sin

Intentionality in one's spiritual walk includes the conscious repudiation of sin. This means not merely avoiding sin as one avoids potholes on a road, but actively fleeing from it, as Joseph fled from Potiphar's wife (Genesis 39). It involves the recognition of sin's destructive power and the conscious decision to pursue holiness.

The Consistent Practice of Spiritual Disciplines

Just as a musician practices scales to play harmoniously, the Christian practices spiritual disciplines to walk in harmony with Jehovah's will. This involves prayer, meditation on the Scriptures, fasting, worship, and other practices that draw one closer to God and fortify the spirit against the snares of the enemy.

The Wise Stewardship of Time

Time is a gift from Jehovah, and how one uses it is a reflection of spiritual priorities. Like the wise builder who counts the cost before building (Luke 14:28), the mindful Christian carefully considers how to allocate time to the service of Jehovah, the edification of others, and personal spiritual growth.

The Cultivation of Godly Relationships

Intentional spiritual conduct extends to the cultivation of relationships that encourage and build up one's faith. The Apostle Paul commends believers to "encourage one another and build one another up" (1 Thessalonians 5:11). This means forming bonds with those who share a love for Jehovah and His Word and who can offer mutual support in the walk of faith.

The Vigilant Guarding Against Worldliness

The Bible admonishes believers not to love the world or the things in the world (1 John 2:15). Walking with intentionality includes vigilant guarding against the insidious creep of worldliness into one's life, which can subtly influence beliefs, attitudes, and behaviors, drawing one away from Jehovah.

The Active Pursuit of Wisdom

Walking in wisdom means seeking Jehovah's guidance in all things and making decisions based on His timeless principles. It is like Solomon, who asked for wisdom to lead Jehovah's people (1 Kings 3:9), understanding that human insight is limited and divine wisdom is necessary for a life that pleases God.

The Patient Endurance in Trials

Mindfulness in spiritual conduct also means patient endurance in the face of trials, recognizing that "the testing of your faith produces steadfastness" (James 1:3). It is to navigate the storms of life with the assurance that Jehovah is sovereign and that He uses such times to refine one's faith.

The Joyful Embrace of God's Sovereignty

Finally, intentional spiritual conduct is characterized by a joyful embrace of Jehovah's sovereignty. It is to walk through life with the confidence of the Psalmist who proclaimed, "The steps of a good man are ordered by Jehovah" (Psalm 37:23), trusting in His perfect plan and timing.

As we reflect on the intentionality of spiritual conduct, it becomes clear that each step taken in faith is a testament to a life lived for Jehovah. To "walk humbly with your God" is not merely an abstract concept but a daily, conscious effort to align one's life with God's purposes and to demonstrate His love and truth to a watching world. Each mindful step is a step towards spiritual maturity, a step taken in the light of His presence, and a step that leads to eternal communion with Him.

Eyes Wide Open: The Conscious Choice to Walk Uprightly

The journey of walking humbly with God is paved with conscious decisions. Every step reflects a choice: to either uphold righteousness or to succumb to the wayward paths that veer off the course set by divine will. To walk uprightly is to live with "eyes wide open," fully aware of the gravity of our choices and the impacts they have, not only on our spiritual health but also on the testimony we bear to the world.

Understanding the Path of Uprightness

To walk uprightly is to navigate life's complexities with a moral compass calibrated by Scripture. It involves a vigilant awareness of the ways in which one's environment, influences, and personal inclinations can lead away from the straight path that Jehovah has delineated for His followers. It is a commitment to seek out and abide by the high standards of character and conduct that the Lord has set forth.

The Visibility of a Godly Walk

Living with spiritual integrity is not a private affair; it is observed by those around us. The upright walk is like a city on a hill, visible to all (Matthew 5:14). When we walk with integrity, we provide a living example of godliness that can draw others towards the truth of God's Word. Our lives become a testament to Jehovah's transformative power, a beacon that can guide others out of darkness.

Choosing Wisdom Over Folly

In a world teeming with distractions and temptations, the choice to walk uprightly is a choice to value wisdom over folly. Just as the Proverbs contrast the path of wisdom with the way of the fool, the believer must discern between actions that lead to life and those that lead to destruction. Upright walking necessitates a continuous selection of wisdom's path, even when folly's road may seem more appealing or convenient.

The Challenge of Upright Living in a Fallen World

Walking uprightly in a fallen world is challenging; it often goes against the current of societal norms and popular opinion. Like Noah, who was "a righteous man, blameless in his generation" (Genesis 6:9), believers are called to maintain their integrity even when it sets them apart. This calls for courage and resilience, grounded in faith that Jehovah values and rewards righteousness.

Integrity in the Mundane

Uprightness is not only about the big decisions but also about the small, everyday choices. It's about being honest when no one is watching, keeping promises even when it costs us, and living out the fruit of the spirit in all circumstances. It is in the mundane aspects of life that the true character is often most clearly seen.

Confronting and Overcoming Sin

The upright walk involves confronting and overcoming sin, not through our own strength, but through the power of the Holy Spirit and the guidance of Scripture. As David sought forgiveness and restoration after his sin with Bathsheba (Psalm 51), so must believers continually return to Jehovah for cleansing and strength to overcome sin's allure.

The Humble Acknowledgment of Dependence on God

Upright living is also characterized by a humble acknowledgment of our dependence on Jehovah. We walk uprightly not by asserting our own righteousness, but by relying on God's grace and guidance. It is an acknowledgment, as the psalmist writes, that "it is God who arms me with strength and makes my way perfect" (Psalm 18:32).

The Active Avoidance of Compromise

The upright walk requires the active avoidance of moral and spiritual compromise. It means not only avoiding overtly sinful behaviors but also guarding against the more subtle forms of compromise that can insinuate themselves into our beliefs and practices. Like Daniel and his friends who refused to defile themselves with the king's food (Daniel 1:8), believers must be vigilant in maintaining their spiritual distinctiveness.

Consistency in Spiritual Disciplines

Consistency in prayer, Bible study, and other spiritual disciplines is vital for the upright walk. These practices keep us anchored in Jehovah's truth and equipped for every good work (2 Timothy 3:17). Through these means, we are reminded of Jehovah's love, strengthened in our faith, and nourished in our spiritual lives.

Relational Integrity

Uprightness extends to our relationships as well. It means speaking truthfully, acting justly, and showing love and compassion in our interactions with others. The Apostle Paul's instructions to "let your speech always be gracious, seasoned with salt" (Colossians 4:6) encapsulate the idea of relational integrity that underpins an upright life.

Commitment to Ongoing Spiritual Growth

Finally, the conscious choice to walk uprightly is a commitment to ongoing spiritual growth. It recognizes that spiritual maturity is not a destination but a journey marked by continual progress and sanctification. As we walk in the light of God's presence, we grow in grace and knowledge of our Lord and Savior (2 Peter 3:18), ever striving to reflect His glory more fully.

Conclusion

The upright walk is a vibrant, intentional journey with Jehovah. It's not simply about avoiding wrongdoing but about actively pursuing a life that mirrors the character and will of God. This path is marked by wise choices, moral courage, and a heart attuned to God's purposes. With eyes wide open to the reality of God's presence and sovereignty, believers are empowered to live lives that not only please Jehovah but also shine forth His righteousness in a world in desperate need of His light.

CHAPTER 18 Walk by the Spirit

Spirit-Led Steps: Aligning with the Divine Presence

The call to walk by the spirit is a central tenet of the Christian life, challenging believers to live in a way that is harmonious with the divine presence of God. This concept encapsulates the essence of a relationship with Jehovah that is active and dynamic, wherein one's life is continually being conformed to the will of God as revealed in the Scriptures. It is a journey that requires dedication, discernment, and a heartfelt desire to embody the principles laid out by the Almighty.

The Heartbeat of the Spirit-Led Life

The spirit-led life is akin to a dance, where the believer must attune themselves to the leading of their divine partner. It is not a solo performance but a collaborative endeavor that harmonizes human will with divine direction. The Spirit does not force His leading upon us but gently guides those who are willing to follow. As Paul expressed in Galatians 5:25, "If we live by the Spirit, let us also keep in step with the Spirit." This invites believers to not only accept the gift of salvation but also to actively participate in the sanctification process.

Recognizing the Voice of the Spirit

Aligning with the divine presence necessitates an acute awareness of the Spirit's voice, which is discerned through the study of Scripture, prayer, and the counsel of mature believers. The Bible is not just a historical document but the living word of Jehovah (Hebrews 4:12), and through it, the Spirit speaks, guides, and corrects. Like Samuel who learned to recognize Jehovah's voice (1 Samuel 3), believers must cultivate a sensitivity to the spiritual nudges that align with scriptural truth.

Yielding to Divine Influence

Yielding to the Spirit means submitting our desires, plans, and actions to God's scrutiny and allowing His will to take precedence over ours. It is reminiscent of Jesus' prayer in the garden of Gethsemane, where He said, "not as I will, but as you will" (Matthew 26:39). This submission is not passive but an active and intentional deference to the leading of the Spirit.

The Practice of Presence

Walking by the Spirit involves the daily practice of God's presence, acknowledging Jehovah in all aspects of life. It requires mindfulness of His nearness in every moment, whether in times of decision-making, in interpersonal relationships, or in personal conduct. It is recognizing, as David did, that one cannot flee from Jehovah's presence (Psalm 139:7-10), and hence, every action is performed as though directly before the eyes of the Almighty.

Conformity to Spiritual Fruit

The fruits of the Spirit enumerated in Galatians 5:22-23 serve as a barometer for the spirit-led life. Love, joy, peace, patience, kindness, goodness, faithfulness, gentleness, and self-control are not merely ethical guidelines but the natural byproduct of a life lived in sync with the Spirit. The cultivation of these virtues is an indicator that a believer is walking in step with the Spirit, as these attributes are not cultivated by human effort alone but are imparted through divine influence.

The Journey Away from the Flesh

As one walks by the Spirit, there is a concurrent journey away from the flesh. The flesh represents the old nature, inclined towards sin and rebellion against God's laws. Paul admonishes believers in Romans 8:13 that if they live according to the flesh they will die, but if by the Spirit they put to death the deeds of the body, they will live. The spirit-led walk is characterized by a turning away from the carnal desires that once dictated behavior, embracing instead a life that is characterized by spiritual vitality and obedience to Jehovah.

Endurance in Adversity

The spirit-led life is not devoid of challenges; however, it is marked by an enduring faith that perseveres through adversity. This endurance is fueled by the hope and strength that the Spirit provides, not as a distant force, but as a present help in times of need (Psalm 46:1). As the Apostle Paul faced hardships, he relied on the strength provided by the Spirit (2 Corinthians 12:9), setting an example for all believers to follow.

Adaptability and Growth

To walk by the Spirit also means to remain adaptable, ready to grow and change direction as Jehovah leads. It is to accept the refining work of the Spirit, which often involves pruning (John 15:2) so that one may bear more fruit. This process is not comfortable, but it is essential for spiritual maturity and deeper communion with God.

Continuous Surrender and Obedience

The spirit-led walk is a continuous cycle of surrender and obedience. Each day presents new opportunities to choose the Spirit's leading over personal inclination. It is a life of habitual yielding to the divine will, a constant echoing of Isaiah's words, "Here am I! Send me" (Isaiah 6:8), reflecting a readiness to follow Jehovah's direction.

In essence, to walk by the Spirit is to live a life that is in constant alignment with Jehovah's presence, will, and purposes. It is to be led by His Word and Spirit in every area of life, ever seeking to reflect His character and fulfill His plans. This walk is not one of solitary endeavor but is undertaken within the community of faith, encouraging and being encouraged by fellow believers. As believers align their steps with the divine presence, they not only experience the fullness of life that Jehovah promises but also become conduits of His grace and truth in a world that is in need of His transformative power.

Invisible Guidance: The Daily Influence of the Spirit on Our Walk

In the Christian journey, the Holy Spirit's guidance is as vital as the compass for the sailor or the map for the hiker. This invisible guidance is ever-present, influencing our walk with subtle nudges, conviction, and comfort. The role of the Spirit is indispensable in leading believers into all truth and enabling them to live out the principles of Scripture in everyday life.

The Whisper of Conviction

The Holy Spirit's influence often comes as a whisper of conviction that echoes the voice of conscience. When faced with moral choices or the temptation to stray from Jehovah's commandments, the Spirit reminds us of the path of righteousness. Consider King David, who, after his sin with Bathsheba, felt the piercing conviction brought on by Jehovah's Spirit through the prophet Nathan (2 Samuel 12). The Spirit's role is not to condemn but to bring to light the things hidden in darkness (1 Corinthians 4:5), prompting us toward repentance and realignment with God's will.

Guidance in Truth

The Spirit's guidance is deeply rooted in truth—specifically, the truth revealed in Scripture. Jesus promised that the Spirit of truth would guide His followers into all truth (John 16:13). This is not a revelation of new truths but a deeper understanding of the truths already revealed in the Bible. The Spirit helps believers to discern the deep things of God, much like how the Spirit revealed to the apostles the mysteries of Christ which they, in turn, taught to the early church (1 Corinthians 2:10).

Counsel in Decision-Making

In decisions both large and small, the Spirit provides counsel that steers believers towards God's purpose for their lives. The account of the Jerusalem Council in Acts 15 is a prime example. The apostles and elders came together to make a significant decision regarding Gentile believers. The conclusion that it seemed good to the Holy Spirit and to them (Acts 15:28) underscores the Spirit's guiding role in the collective and individual decision-making of God's people.

Comfort in Trials

As a comforter, the Holy Spirit sustains believers through trials, offering peace that surpasses human understanding (Philippians 4:7). This comfort is not an abstract feeling but a real and present help in times of need (Psalm 46:1). It is the same comfort that was promised by Jesus and experienced by Paul, who referred to God as "the Father of mercies and God of all comfort" (2 Corinthians 1:3-4).

Empowerment for Service

The influence of the Spirit is also evident in the empowerment for service. Throughout the Acts of the Apostles, we see the Spirit enabling believers to proclaim the message of Christ boldly, regardless of the circumstances. The Spirit gave the disciples the words to speak before rulers and authorities (Luke 12:12), just as the Spirit empowers believers today to witness and serve in various capacities within the body of Christ.

The Fruit of the Spirit

In the believer's character, the fruit of the Spirit—love, joy, peace, patience, kindness, goodness, faithfulness, gentleness, and self-control—is a testament to the Spirit's transformative work (Galatians 5:22-23). These virtues are not the result of human effort but of the Spirit's cultivation in the life of a believer who remains connected to Christ, much like branches to a vine (John 15:4-5).

Prompting to Prayer

The Spirit prompts believers to engage in prayer, sometimes interceding with groans that words cannot express (Romans 8:26-27). This intercessory role is a powerful aspect of the Spirit's guidance, especially when believers are uncertain of Jehovah's will. It is an assurance that even when words fail, the Spirit communicates the sincere desires of the heart to God.

Confirmation of Sonship

One of the most profound influences of the Spirit is the confirmation of our sonship with God. "The Spirit himself bears witness with our spirit that we are children of God" (Romans 8:16). This assurance is crucial for the believer's identity, informing every aspect of their walk with God.

Prophetic Insight

While the complete canon of Scripture provides the final authoritative prophetic revelation, the Spirit can grant insight into the application of these prophecies in the contemporary world. Such insight always aligns with the Bible and serves to edify the believer, helping them to discern the times and seasons in light of biblical truth.

Sanctification in Truth

Ultimately, the daily influence of the Spirit is directed towards sanctification—the process by which believers are set apart for God's holy purposes. As Jesus prayed for His disciples, "Sanctify them in the truth; your word is truth" (John 17:17), so the Spirit works to sanctify believers, using the truth of Scripture as the standard.

Conclusion

In summary, the daily influence of the Spirit on our walk with God is multifaceted and profound. It encompasses conviction, comfort, counsel, empowerment, and much more, always aligning with and pointing back to the truth of Scripture. Through the Spirit's guidance, believers are equipped to navigate the complexities of life while maintaining their course toward the ultimate destination: conformity to the image of Christ for the glory of Jehovah.

Bibliography

Akin, D. L. (2001). *The New American Commentary: 1, 2, 3 John.* Nashville, TN: Broadman & Holman .

Aland, K., Black, M., & Martini, C. M. (1993; 2006). *The Greek New Testament, Fourth Revised Edition (Interlinear With Morphology).* Deutsche Bibelgesellschaft: United Bible Society.

Alden, R. L. (2001). *Job, The New American Commentary, vol. 11* . Nashville: Broadman & Holman Publishers.

Anders, M. (1999). *Holman New Testament Commentary: vol. 8, Galatians-Colossians* . Nashville, TN: Broadman & Holman Publishers.

Anders, M. (1999). *Holman New Testament Commentary: vol. 8, Galatians, Ephesians, Philippians, Colossians.* Nashville, TN: Broadman & Holman Publishers.

Anders, M. (2005). *Holman Old Testament Commentary - Proverbs* . Nashville: B&H Publishing.

Anders, M., & Butler, T. (2002). *Holman Old Testament Commentary: Isaiah.* Nashiville, TN: B&H Publishing.

Anders, M., & Lawson, S. (2004). *Holman Old Testament Commentary - Psalms: 11.* Grand Rapids: B&H Publishing.

Anders, M., & McIntosh, D. (2009). *Holman Old Testament Commentary - Deuteronomy.* Nashville: B&H Publishing.

Andrews, E. (2016). *Misrepresenting Jesus: Debunking Bart D. Ehrman's Misquoting Jesus [Second Edition].* Cambridge: Christian Publishing House.

Andrews, E. D. (2015). *CRISIS OF FAITH: Saving Those Who Doubt* . Cambridge, OH: Christian Publishing House.

Andrews, E. D. (2016). *INTERPRETING THE BIBLE: Introduction to Biblical Hermeneutics.* Cambridge, OH: Christian Publishing House.

Andrews, E. D. (2016). *YOUR WORD IS TRUTH: Being Sanctified In the Truth.* Cambridge, OH: Christian Publishing House.

Andrews, E. D. (2017). *HUMAN IMPERFECTION: While We Were Sinners Christ Died For Us.* Cambridge, OH: Christian Ppublishing House.

Andrews, E. D. (2017). *TURN OLD HABITS INTO NEW HABITS: Why and How the Bible Makes a Difference.* Cambridge, OH: Christian Publishing House.

Andrews, E. D. (2017). *YOU CAN MAKE A DIFFERENCE: Why and How Your Christian Life Makes a Difference.* Cambridge, OH: Christian Publishing House.

Andrews, E. D. (2018). *LET GOD USE YOU TO SOLVE YOUR PROBLEMS: GOD Will Instruct You and Teach You In the Way You Should Go.* Cambridge, OH: Christian Publishing House.

Andrews, E. D. (2018). *THE POWER OF GOD: The Word That Will Change Your Life Today.* Cambridge, OH: Christian Publishing House.

Andrews, E. D. (2018). *WHY ME?: When Bad Things Happen to Good People.* Cambridge, OH: Christian Publishing House.

Andrews, E. D. (2019). *SATAN: Know Your Enemy.* Cambridge, OH: Christian Publishing House.

Andrews, E. D. (2022). *THE LETTER OF JAMES: An Apologetic and Background Exposition of the Holy Scriptures (CPH New Testament Commentary).* Cambridge, Ohio: Christian Publishing House.

Andrews, E. D. (2023). *BIBLICAL EXEGESIS: Biblical Criticism on Trial.* Cambridge, OH: Christian Publishing House.

Andrews, E. D. (2023). *CHRISTIAN APOLOGETICS: Answering the Tough Questions: Evidence and Reason in Defense of the Faith.* Cambridge, Ohio: Christian Publishing House.

Andrews, E. D. (2023). *FAITHFUL MINDS: A Biblical and Cognitive Behavioral Therapy Approach to Mental Health and Wellness.* Cambridge, OH: Christian Publishing House.

Andrews, E. D. (2023). *LIFE DOES HAVE A PURPOSE: Discovering and Living Your Ultimate Purpose.* Cambridge, OH: Christian Publishing House.

Andrews, E. D. (2023). *MERE CHRISTIANITY REIMAGINED: Rediscovering the Faith for the 21st Century.* Cambridge, OH: Christian Publishing House.

Andrews, E. D. (2023). *THE BOOK OF PROVERBS Chapters 1-15: CPH Old Testament Commentary: Volume 17.* Cambridge, OH: Christian Publishing House.

Andrews, E. D. (2023). *THE BOOK OF PROVERBS Chapters 16-23: CPH Old Testament Commentary: Volume 18*. Cambridge, OH: Christian Publishing House.

Andrews, E. D. (2023). *THE EXPOSITORY DICTIONARY: A Companion Study Tool to the Updated American Standard Version*. Cambridge, OH: Christian Publishing House.

Andrews, E. D. (2023). *UNSHAKABLE BELIEFS: Strategies for Strengthening and Defending Your Faith*. Cambridge, OH: Christian Publishing House.

Andrews, E. D., & Marshall, T. F. (2023). *PAUL'S LETTER TO THE EPHESIANS: CPH New Testament Commentary*. Cambridge, OH: Christian Publishing House.

Andrews, S. J., & Bergen, R. D. (2009). *Holman Old Testament Commentary: 1-2 Samuel*. Nashville: Broadman & Holman.

Arndt, W., Danker, F. W., & Bauer, W. (2000). *A Greek-English Lexicon of the New Testament and Other Early Christian Literature. 3rd ed.* . Chicago: University of Chicago Press.

Arnold, C. E. (2002). *Zondervan Illustrated Bible Backgrounds Commentary Volume 4: Hebrews to Revelation*. Grand Rapids, MI: Zondervan.

Barclay, W. (1974). *New Testament Words*. Louisville: Westminster Press.

Barker, K. L., & Bailey, W. (2001). *The New American Commentary: vol. 20, Micah, Nahum, Habakkuk, Zephaniah*. Nashville, TN: Broadman & Holman Publishers.

Benner, D. G., & Hill, P. C. (1985, 1999). *Baker Encyclopedia of Psychology and Counseling (Second Edition)*. Grand Rapids: Baker Books.

Bercot, D. W. (1998). *A Dictionary of Early Christian Beliefs*. Peabody: Hendrickson.

Bettenson, H., & Maunder, C. (1999). *Documents of the Christian Church, 3rd. ed.* Oxford : Oxford University Press.

Bland, D. (2002). *The College Press NIV Commentary: Proverbs, Ecclesiastes & Song of Songs,* . Joplin: College Press Pub. Co.

Blomberg, C. (1992). *The New American Commentary: Matthew*. Nashville, TN: Broadman & Holman Publishers.

Boa, K., & Kruidenier, W. (2000). *Holman New Testament Commentary: Romans*. Nashville: Broadman & Holman.

Bock, D. L. (1994). *Baker Exegetical Commentary on the New Testament: Luke Volume 1: 1:1-9:50*. Grand Rapids, Mich: Baker Books.

Borchert, G. L. (2001). *The New American Commentary: John 1-11* . Nashville, TN: Broadman & Holman Publishers.

Borchert, G. L. (2002). *The New American Commentary vol. 25B, John 12–21*. Nashville: Broadman & Holman Publishers.

Brand, C., Draper, C., & Archie, E. (2003). *Holman Illustrated Bible Dictionary: Revised, Updated and Expanded*. Nashville, TN: Holman.

Bromiley, G. W. (1986). *The International Standard Bible Encyclopedia (Vol. 1-4)*. Grand Rapids, MI: William B. Eerdmans Publishing Co.

Brooks, J. A. (1992). *The New American Commentary: Mark (Volume 23)*. Nashville: Broadman & Holman Publishers.

Bruce, F. F. (1977). *New Testament History*. New York: Doubleday.

Butler, T. C. (2000). *Holman New Testament Commentary: Luke*. Nashville, TN: Broadman & Holman Publishers.

Butler, T. C. (2005). *Holman Old Testament Commentary - Hosea, Joel, Amos, Obadiah, Jonah, Micah* . Nashville: Broadman & Holman Publishers.

Cameron, K., & Comfort, R. (2004). *The School of Biblical Evangelism: 101 Lessons: How to Share Your Faith Simply, Effectively, Biblically—the Way Jesus Did*. Gainesville, FL: Bridge-Logos Publishers.

Carson, D. A. (1991). *The Gospel According to John*. Grand Rapids, MI: William B. Eerdmans Publishing Company.

Comfort, P. W. (2008). *New Testament Text and Translation Commentary*. Carol Stream: Tyndale House Publishers.

Cooper, R. (2000). *Holman New Testament Commentary: Mark*. Nashville: Broadman & Holman Publishers.

Easley, K. H. (1998). *Holman New Testament Commentary, vol. 12, Revelation*. (Nashville, TN: Broadman & Holman Publishers.

Ehrman, B. D. (2005). *Misquoting Jesus: The Story Behind Who Changed the Bible and Why*. New York: Harper One.

Elwell, W. A. (2001). *Evangelical Dictionary of Theology (Second Edition)*. Grand Rapids: Baker Academic.

Erickson, M. J. (2001). *The Concise Dictionary of Christian Theology*. Wheaton: Crossway Books.

Fields, L. M. (2008). *Hebrew For The Rest of Us: Using Hebrew Tools Without Mastering Biblical Hebrew*. Grand Rapids, MI: Zondervan.

Gamble, H. Y. (1995). *Books and Readers in the Early Church: A History of Early Christian Texts*. New Haven: New Haven University Press.

Gangel, K. O. (1998). *Holman New Testament Commentary: Acts*. Nashville, TN: Broadman & Holman Publishers.

Gangel, K. O. (2000). *Holman New Testament Commentary, vol. 4, John* . Nashville, TN: Broadman & Holman Publishers.

Garrett, D. A. (1993). *Proverbs, Ecclesiastes, Song of Songs, The New American Commentary, vol. 14*. Nashville: Broadman & Holman Publishers.

George, T. (2001). *The New American Commentary: Galatians* . Nashville, TN: Broadman & Holman Publishers.

Green, J. B., McKnight, S., & Marshall, H. (1992). *Dictionary of Jesus and the Gospels*. Downers Grove, IL: InterVarsity Press.

Harris, R. L., Archer, G. L., & Waltke, B. K. (1999, c1980). *Theological Wordbook of the Old Testament*. Chicago: Moody Press.

Hill, C. E., & Kruger, M. J. (2012). *The Early Text of the New Testament*. Oxford: Oxford University Press.

Hill, J. (2006). *Zondervan Handbook to the History of Christianity*. Oxford: Lion.

Kistemaker, S. J., & Hendriksen, W. (1953-2001). *New Testament Commentary: Exposition of the Acts of the Apostles* . Grand Rapids, MI: Baker Book House.

Lange, J. P., Schaff, P., Moll, C. B., & Kendrick, A. C. (2008). *A Commentary on the Holy Scriptures: Hebrews*. Bellingham, WA: Logos Bible Software.

Larson, K. (2000). *Holman New Testament Commentary, vol. 9, I & II Thessalonians, I & II Timothy, Titus, Philemon*. Nashville, TN: Broadman & Holman Publishers.

Lea, T. D. (1999). *Holman New Testament Commentary: Hebrews, James*. Nashville, TN: Broadman & Holman Publishers.

Lea, T. D., & Griffin, H. P. (1992). *The New American Commentary, vol. 34, 1, 2 Timothy, Titus.* Nashville: Broadman & Holman Publishers.

Lenski, R. C. (1942, 2008). *The Interpretation of St. John's Gospel.* Minneapolis: Augsburg Fortress.

Little, P. E. (2008). *Know What You Believe*. Downers Grove. ILL: InterVarsity Press.

MacArthur, J. (2005). *The MacArthur Bible Commentary.* Nashville: Thomas Nelson.

Marshall, T. F., & Andrews, E. D. (2022). *PAUL'S LETTER TO THE PHILIPPIANS: An Apologetic and Background Exposition of the Holy Scriptures.* Cambridge, Ohio: Christian publishing House.

Martin, D. M. (2001, c1995). *The New American Commentary 33 1, 2 Thessalonians* . Nashville, TN: Broadman & Holman.

Martin, G. S. (2002). *Holman Old Testament Commentary: Numbers.* Nashville: Broadman & Holman Publishers.

Mathews, K. A. (2001). *The New American Commentary vol. 1A, Genesis 1-11:26* . Nashville: Broadman & Holman Publishers.

Melick, R. R. (2001). *The New American Commentary: vol. 32, Philippians, Colissians, Philemon.* Nashville, TN : Broadman & Holman Publishers.

Miller, S. R. (1994). *The New American Commentary: Volume 18 Daniel.* Nashville: Broadman & Holman Publishers.

Moulton, J. H., & Howard, W. F. (1908). *A Grammar of New Testament Greek, Volume 1.* Edinburgh: T & T Clark.

Mounce, R. H. (2001, c1995). *Romans: The New American Commentary 27.* Nashville: Broadman & Holman.

Mounce, W. D. (2006). *Mounce's Complete Expository Dictionary of Old & New Testament Words.* Grand Rapids, MI: Zondervan.

Myers, A. C. (1987). *The Eerdmans Bible Dictionary* . Grand Rapids, Mich: Eerdmans.

Nicoll, W. R. (1956). *The Expositor's Greek New Testament: Vol IV.* Peabody, MA: Hendrickson.

Oden, T. C. (1989). *Ministry Through Word and Sacrament, Classic Pastoral Care.* New York: Crossroad.

Polhill, J. B. (2001). *The New American Commentary 26: Acts.* Nashville: Broadman & Holman Publishers.

Pratt Jr, R. L. (2000). *Holman New Testament Commentary: I & II Corinthians, vol. 7.* Nashville: Broadman & Holman Publishers.

Richardson, K. (1997). *The New American Commentary Vol. 36 James.* Nashville: Broadman & Holman Publishers.

Robertson, A. (1997). *Word Pictures in the New Testament.* Oak Harbor, MI: Logos Research Systems.

Rooker, M. F. (2000). *The New American Commentary, vol. 3A, Leviticus.* Nashville: Broadman & Holman Publishers.

Scholars, 2. B. (2006). *Biblical Studies Press, The NET Bible First Edition Notes, Proverbs.* Richardson: Biblical Studies Press.

Schreiner, T. R. (2003). *The New American Commentary: 1, 2 Peter, Jude.* Nashville: Broadman & Holman.

Smith, G. (2007). *The New American Commentary: Isaiah 1-39, Vol. 15a.* Nashville, TN: B & H Publishing Group.

Smith, G. (2009). *The New American Commentary: Isaiah 40-66, Vol. 15b.* Nashville, TN: B&H Publishing.

Stein, R. H. (2001, c1992). *The New American Commentary: Luke.* Nashville, TN: Broadman & Holman .

Stuart, D. K. (2006). *The New American Commentary: An Exegetical Theological Exposition of Holy Scripture EXODUS.* Nashville: Broadman & Holman.

Thomas, R. L. (1992). *Revelation 1-7: An Exegetical Commentary .* Chicago, IL: Moody Publishers.

Thomas, R. L. (1995). *Revelation 8-22: An Exegetical Commentary .* Chicago, IL: Moody Publishers.

Tozer, A. (1993). *The Pursuit of God: The Human Thirst for the Divine.* Camp Hill, PA: Christian Publications, Inc.

Vine, W. E. (1996). *Vine's Expository Dictionary of Old and New Testament Words.* Nashville: Thomas Nelson.

Wallace, D. (1996). *Greek Grammar Beyond the Basics.* Grad Rapids: Zondervan.

Walls, D., & Anders, M. (1996). *Holman New Testament Commentary: I & II Peter, I, II & III John, Jude.* Nashville: Broadman & Holman Publishers.

Watson, R. (1832). *A Biblical and Theological Dictionary: Explanatory of the History, Manners and Customs of the Jews.* New York: Waugh and T. Mason.

Weber, S. K. (2000). *Holman New Testament Commentary, vol. 1, Matthew.* Nashville, TN: Broadman & Holman Publishers.

Wood, D. R. (1996). *New Bible Dictionary (Third Edition).* Downers Grove: InterVarsity Press.

www.ingramcontent.com/pod-product-compliance
Lightning Source LLC
Chambersburg PA
CBHW070448050426
42451CB00015B/3399